DARK PSYCHOLOGY

THE BEGINNERS GUIDE TO MASTER COVERT MANIPULATION, DISCOVER THE DARK SIDE OF COMMUNICATION AND TO LEARN PERSUASION SKILLS AND THE SECRETS OF HUMAN PSYCHOLOGY

professional advice. The content within this book has been derived from various sources. Please consult a licensed professional before attempting any techniques outlined in this book.

By reading this document, the reader agrees that under no circumstances is the author responsible for any losses, direct or indirect, which are incurred as a result of the use of information contained within this document, including, but not limited to, — errors, omissions, or inaccuracies.

Table of Contents

Introduction

In our world, we need to start to become more aware of manipulation. When you can recognize that someone is trying to control you, it will be much easier to stay out of their controlling grasp.

When you start to better identify manipulation, how it develops, and how it has affected your life, then it will only become easier to navigate without it. Interacting with others can include doing your best to avoid it healthily. However, stopping ourselves from being manipulated isn't the only important thing we will be discussing.

We will pay significant attention to how you can become a persuasive person yourself. Though you might have been hurt in the past by manipulation, or even damaged your mental health by being the manipulator yourself, there is hope, now that we can work towards a better future for ourselves. This is done by becoming an inspirational and potentially influential person.

Manipulation is dangerous, but when it is put in a more positive light, it can become healthy influence.

If you are able to be a persuasive individual and not only get what you want, but fulfill the needs of others as well, then it will become easier for you to be able to get the things that you desire the most in life.

Rather than always doing things you don't enjoy, being the "yes man," or letting people take advantage of your good nature, you can become just as influential as the people who have tried to control you previously.

You might even be at a point where you fear manipulation altogether. Why would you want to do something to others that has actually caused you grief in the past? This kind of thinking is because we have only been aware of the negative types of manipulation. Not only that, but it is important to ensure we have the tools to understand how to get these things.

The first important step in this process is to investigate the personality types of manipulators, as well as the people whom they commonly go after. You may have heard of the common personality type, "Narcissist," a person who is only concerned with himself and getting the things he wants. Narcissists might take advantage of empaths, or highly sensitive people who are more concerned with the wellbeing of others.

After that, we will further explore positive manipulative personalities and the way that you can adopt some of these helpful practices in your own relationships.

Aside from that, we will also be discovering how our bodies communicate, the signals and responses that we give off, and what others might be taking away from our body language. The better you can understand influence through ways besides our verbal communication, the easier it will be to avoid becoming influenced yourself and to better persuade those around you.

After we understand what all of this means, it will be easier to learn and practice the rest of the influential tips that we will be sharing throughout the book. Though it might seem easier to negatively manipulate those from whom you want something, the person whom you would be hurting most in this process is going to be yourself.

Always look for ways of positive influence so that you can mutually benefit both parties.

Chapter 1: understand human psychology

Psychology is generally accepted as the scientific study of the mind and human behavior. It focuses on the mind, how the mind functions, and also how it influences or affects behavior. "Psychology" is a word that comes from the Greek words "psyche" and "logo." Psyche means or translates to "life," while logos means "explanation."

The mind is very complex, and so are the things that are related to it, which can make it hard to treat. Psychology encompasses all facets of the human experience, ranging from the workings and functions of the brain to the decisions and actions of nations. This even includes the development of a child and the care given or received by the aged. It encompasses the process of thoughts, memories, emotions, dreams, behavior, perception, and many more that cannot be physically seen but understood.

The subject psychology covers the study of both the conscious and the unconscious occurrences including thought and feeling. Psychology is also an academic discipline with a very broad scope. It pursues the understanding of the evolving properties and workings of the brain. As a social science, psychology pursues the understanding of both groups and individuals by researching particular cases and instituting broad-spectrum principles.

A psychologist is a professional researcher or practitioner in any field of psychology, and they are classified as behaviorists, cognitive psychologists, or social scientists. Psychologists aim to understand the function of the human mind, behavior, and mental processes ranging from attention, cognition, perception, intelligence, emotions, phenomenology, brain-functioning, decision-making, morality, relationships, motivation, and even personality.

Psychology has been acclaimed to be the "core science." In medical science, it leans toward psychiatry and neurology, while in the social sciences, it leans toward human behavior, development, experiences, and other subdisciplines within psychology.

Although psychological knowledge is habitually used for the assessment and treatment of issues related to mental health, it is also applied every day in several other spheres of human endeavors. This includes understanding and solving different types of problems, such as solving mysteries and problems in crime dramas on television. Psychology, in the long run, aims to benefit and advance society.

Most psychologists are engaged in different roles, from practicing in clinics, managing a therapeutic practice, counseling, or practicing in school settings. Other psychologists engage in a wide range of scientific research covering broad areas such as mental processes and behavior. Some provide services to psychology departments in universities, including teaching hospitals and medical schools. Other psychologists are employed to provide professional services in large organizations and in government settings. Finally, other settings where you might find a psychologist include a forensic investigation department, law agencies, human development and aging, media, health, and sports as well as in the military and intelligence.

Emotions

Our emotions appear to be in control of our daily lives. The decisions we make are based on whether we are sad, happy, angry, frustrated, or bored. The hobbies and activities we choose to partake in are incited by our emotions. Moving through our daily lives, we get to experience a variety of emotions.

What are emotions? Emotions are complex psychological states that encompass three different components: a subjective experience, a behavioral or expressive response, and a physiological response. Adding to the definition of emotions, researchers have been able to identify and classify emotions into types. However, these descriptions and insights appear to be changing over time.

Emotion is a subjective state of being, which we often describe as feelings. Emotion and mood are sometimes used interchangeably, but psychologists have pointed out that these words mean two different things. Basically, the word emotion denotes a subjective affective state which is relatively intense and occurs in response to what we experience. Emotions are experienced intentionally and consciously. On the other hand, mood refers to a less intense, prolonged, affective state which doesn't occur in response to what we experience. The state of mood may not be consciously experienced and may not carry the consciousness/intentionality that is associated with emotion. In this section, we will be focusing on human emotion.

Our emotions are essential to our ability to adapt to life's challenges. When we have a good feeling, we are able to shrug off even the biggest of tasks, but when we feel troubled or worried, we tend to see an enjoyable task as too burdensome and view it with a sense of doom and gloom. Our emotions can even go beyond and affect our relationships with other people. For example, if a friend is telling you a sad story and expects you to respond looking sad or concerned, but you choose to look unconcerned and snicker instead, you will only appear rude and insensitive. Likewise, if you are frowning when a friend is telling you of a very funny joke, you will also appear offensive and uninterested.

Going off the handle just because of a minor annoyance can make you appear unbalanced or too hyper. If you give an undue happy reaction to information tagged as good news, people will start to question your stability and maturity. If it was a baby, they are totally allowed to wail with rage and shriek with pleasure at any time, but as an adult, people expect you to rein in the outward expression of your feelings. Our emotions play an important role in our ability to succeed or fail in the challenges thrown at us. Just think about the famous people whose careers have taken a step back because of the way their feelings were expressed. For example, during the primary run-up to the 2004 United States presidential election, the candidacy of Howard Dean ended overnight after his "YAAAAHHH" moment became an internet frenzy. Prior to that, Edmund Muskie made the same political blunder during the 1972 primary season. Muskie shed tears after he won the New Hampshire primary. However, he claimed the tears were snowflakes that were shimmering in the morning light. In the same light, Hillary Clinton wasn't seen as a sympathetic fellow until she had her eyes wet when answering a voter's question. Of course, some pundits used that act against her and questioned her sincerity. You might be asking what these examples have to do with the role of emotions in our lives.

The above examples show us that the outward display of our inner feelings has the power to influence how we are treated by others. Meanwhile, these emotional displays are greatly dependent on our cultural norms. To be recognized as a well-adapted member of society, it is important that we adhere to the norms or risk ridicule or condemnation from other people.

According to the findings of psychologist Paul Ekman in 1972, there are six basic emotions that are recognized widely. These are happiness, sadness, fear, anger, surprise, and disgust. The way in which people express these emotions differs quite radically based on the norms of everyone's culture. In 1999, Ekman expanded his list of basic emotions and included a number of others, including excitement, embarrassment, contempt, pride, shame, amusement, and satisfaction.

Prominent psychologist Robert Plutchik also introduced an emotion classification he called the "wheel of emotions." This model of emotion classification shows how different emotion types can be combined or mixed together just like a color wheel where primary colors are mixed to make other colors.

Chapter 2: Dark personality and dark triad - Machiavellianism, Narcissism, Psychopathy

Dark psychology is not a single, universally applicable medical diagnosis that can be applied across all cases of deviant personalities. There are, in fact, a wide variety of ways that dark psychology may manifest itself in someone's psychological and behavioral makeup. There is no absolute division of one deviant personality type from another, and many deviant personalities with prominent features of dark psychology may display elements of more than one manifestation of dark psychology.

This chapter will explore three types of dark psychology personalities. It is important to remember that although the internet has spawned a huge growth in problems resulting from dark psychology, these traits have been part of human culture since ancient times. In fact, one of the dark psychology profiles we will explore in this chapter, Machiavellianism, takes its name from a medieval politician. Another, narcissism, takes its name from an ancient mythological character. Together, the three dark psychology profiles discussed in this chapter—psychopathy, Machiavellianism, and narcissism—make up what is known as "the Dark Triad."

Psychopathy

Psychopathy is defined as a mental disorder with several identifying characteristics that include antisocial behavior, amorality, an inability to develop empathy or to establish meaningful personal relationships, extreme egocentricity, and recidivism, with repeated violations resulting from an apparent inability to learn from the consequences of earlier transgressions. Antisocial behavior, in turn, is defined as behavior based upon a goal of violating formal and/or informal rules of social conduct through criminal activity or through acts of personal, private protest, or opposition, all of which is directed against other individuals or society in general.

Egocentricity is behavior is when the offending person sees himself or herself as the central focus of the world, or at least of all dominant social and political activity. Empathy is the ability to view and understand events, thoughts, emotions, and beliefs from the perspective of others, and is considered one of the most important psychological components for establishing successful, ongoing relationships.

Amorality is entirely different from immorality. An immoral act is an act which violates established moral codes. A person who is immoral can be confronted with his or her actions with the expectation that he or she will recognize that his or her actions are offensive form a moral, if not a legal, standpoint. Amorality, on the other hand, represents a psychology that does not recognize that any moral codes exist, or if they do, that they have no value in determining whether or not to act in one way or another.

Thus, someone displaying psychopathy may commit horrendous acts that cause tremendous psychological and physical trauma and not ever understand that what he or she has done is wrong. Worse still, those who display signs of psychopathy usually worsen over time because they are unable to make the connection between the problems in their lives and in the lives of those in the world around them and their own harmful and destructive actions.

Machiavellianism

Strictly defined, Machiavellianism is the political philosophy of Niccolò Machiavelli, who lived from 1469 until 1527 in Italy. In contemporary society, Machiavellianism is a term used to describe the popular understanding of people who are perceived as displaying very high political or professional ambitions. In psychology, however, the Machiavellianism scale is used to measure the degree to which people with deviant personalities display manipulative behavior.

Machiavelli wrote The Prince, a political treatise in which he stated that sincerity, honesty, and other virtues were certainly admirable qualities, but that in politics, the capacity to engage in deceit, treachery, and other forms of criminal behavior were acceptable if there were no other means of achieving political aims to protect one's interests.

Popular misconceptions reduce this entire philosophy to the view that "the end justifies the means." To be fair, Machiavelli himself insisted that the more important part of this equation was ensuring that the end itself must first be justified.

Furthermore, it is better to achieve such ends using means devoid of treachery whenever possible because there is less risk to the interests of the actor.

Thus, seeking the most effective means of achieving a political end may not necessarily lead to the most treacherous. In addition, not all political ends that have been justified as worth pursuing must be pursued. In many cases, the mere threat that a certain course of action may be pursued may be enough to achieve that end. In some cases, the treachery may be as mild as making a credible threat to take action that is not really even intended.

In contemporary society, many people overlook the fact that Machiavellianism is part of the "Dark Triad" of dark psychology and tacitly approve of the deviant behavior of political and business leaders who are able to amass great power or wealth. However, as a psychological disorder, Machiavellianism is entirely different from a chosen path to political power.

The person displaying Machiavellian personality traits does not consider whether his or her actions are the most effective means to achieving his or her goals, whether there are alternatives that do not involve deceit or treachery, or even whether the ultimate result of his or her actions is worth achieving. The Machiavellian personality is not evidence of a strategic or calculating mind attempting to achieve a worthwhile objective in a contentious environment. Instead, it is always on, whether the situation calls for a cold, calculating, and manipulative approach or not.

For example, we have all called in sick to work when we really just wanted a day off. But for most of us, such conduct is not how we behave normally, and after such acts of dishonesty, many of us feel guilty. Those who display a high degree of Machiavellianism would not just lie when they want a day off; they see lying and dishonesty as the only way to conduct themselves in all situations, regardless of whether doing so results in any benefit.

What's more, because of the degree of social acceptance and tacit approval granted to Machiavellian personalities who successfully attain political power, their presence in society does not receive the kind of negative attention accorded to the other two members of the Dark Triad—psychopathy and narcissism.

Narcissism

The term "narcissism" originates from an ancient Greek myth about Narcissus, a young man who saw his reflection in a pool of water and fell in love with the image of himself. In clinical psychology, narcissism as an illness was introduced by Sigmund Freud and has continually been included in official diagnostic manuals as a description of a specific type of psychiatric personality disorder.

In psychology, narcissism is defined as a condition characterized by an exaggerated sense of importance, an excessive need for attention, a lack of empathy, and, as a result, dysfunctional relationships. Commonly, narcissists may outwardly display an extremely high level of confidence, but this façade usually hides a very fragile ego and a high degree of sensitivity to criticism. There is often a large gulf between a narcissist's highly favorable view of himself or herself, the resulting expectation that others should extend to him or her favors and special treatment, and the disappointment when the results are quite negative or otherwise different. These problems can affect all areas of the narcissist's life, including personal relationships, professional relationships, and financial matters.

As part of the Dark Triad, those who exhibit traits resulting from Narcissistic Personality Disorder (NPD) may engage in relationships characterized by a lack of empathy. For example, a narcissist may demand constant comments, attention, and admiration from his or her partner, but will often appear unable or unwilling to reciprocate by displaying concern or responding to the concerns, thoughts, and feelings of his or her partner.

Narcissists also display a sense of entitlement and expect excessive reward and recognition, but usually without ever having accomplished or achieved anything that would justify such feelings. There is also a tendency toward excessive criticism of those around him or her, combined with heightened sensitivity when even the slightest amount of criticism is directed at him or her.

Thus, while narcissism in popular culture is often used as a pejorative term and an insult aimed at people like actors, models, and other celebrities who display high degrees of self-love and satisfaction, NPD is actually a psychological term that is quite distinct from merely having high self-esteem. The key to understanding this aspect of dark psychology is that the narcissist's image of himself or herself is often completely and entirely idealized, grandiose, and inflated and cannot be justified with any factual, meaningful accomplishments or capacities that may make such claims believable. As a result of this discord between expectation and reality, the demanding, manipulative, inconsiderate, self-centered, and arrogant behavior of the narcissist can cause problems not only for himself or herself, but for all of the people in his or her life.

The Dark Triad in Practice

The professional workplace has acknowledged the presence of people exhibiting Dark Triad characteristics. The following diagram illustrates that they are tolerated for their efficiency and their ability to get things done but contrasts that ability with the negative effects it has on their ability to form personal relationships:

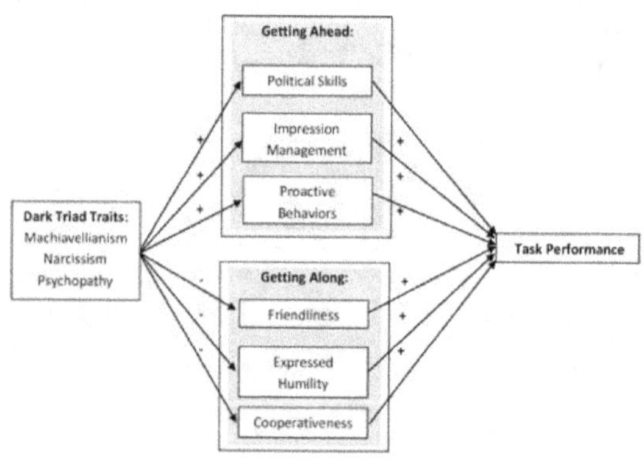

(McLarty, 2015)

The remainder of this book discusses a wide variety of people and situations in which you may find one, two, all three, or some combination of these Dark Triad personalities working in concert around you.

The clinical descriptions are easy enough to categorize, and in isolation, it can be fairly straightforward to separate one type of dark psychology from another. The real world is a lot messier. Many of us have grown accustomed to so-called "toxic relationships," whether they are relationships with our partners, our co-workers, our family members, our bosses, or our political and community leaders. In addition, manifestations of dark psychology are often far more mundane than the dramatic examples we see in major television and film productions about the romantic lives of serial killers and other criminals. The more we accept these relationships as normal, the more difficult it will be to identify them as problematic.

Remember that psychological, emotional, and social predators do not think of themselves as sick. Their lack of morality and empathy, and their adaption form a very early age to live according to rules and methods you may find horribly wrong, can make their presence intimidating. However, you should also remember that even when their amorality and lack of empathy may allow them to enjoy an unjust advantage in relationships, their mental capacities are the result of underdevelopment, not a higher evolutionary state.

Chapter 3: Powerful communication techniques

Communication, quite simply, is defined as the exchanging of information that we do amongst ourselves and other individuals. This exchange of information can take place in the form of speaking, writing, signs, signals or behavior.

If you live in this world, you need to relate to others around you. Nobody can survive without having their needs met, and to have our needs met, whether we like it or not, requires the help of other individuals to do so. And therefore, we need to rely on communication to get by.

Communication is a skill that many don't think twice about, but it is one of the most important skills you could have at your disposal. If you want to know what it is like not to be able to communicate or be understood, just picture a time when you have gone to a foreign country where you do not speak the local language.

Everything suddenly becomes more difficult, doesn't it? You struggle to understand and to make yourself understood, and even simple forms of communication like asking for directions seems like an impossible task. Communication, both verbal and nonverbal, matters. It matters because it helps us relate and collaborate with the people living in the world with us.

There are several reasons why it is important to have effective communication in our everyday life, and those reasons include:

Effective Communication Helps Us Form Relationships

 The foundation of all human relationships is how well you can bond with another person. Two people start off as strangers, and how do they form a bond from there? They start communicating. They interact, they start talking and start getting to know one another and slowly, a relationship begins to form, and it begins with being able to communicate effectively with one another.

Effective Communication Helps Express Ideas & Pass Information

Think of all the greatest inventions that we have in our lives today. All of those came to fruition because the inventors were able to communicate their brilliant ideas to the rest of the world. Effective communication is the reason people can facilitate the process of information and knowledge sharing so seamlessly. Without it, a lot of our ideas, thoughts, and points of view would just be trapped inside our head, and we would not know what to do about it. If you can effectively master the art of communication and make it easy for people to understand, your chances of conveying the information without the danger of being completely misinterpreted will increase that much more.

Effective Communication Avoids Misunderstanding

We all know what happens when information is misunderstood or taken out of context. Heated arguments arise, fights happen, and sometimes relationships get severed because misunderstood information causes hurt feelings or hit a sore spot with someone. That is another major reason why effective communication is such a vital skill to possess. You exist in this world; you need to be able to express your messages clearly and to the point to minimize the chances that what you are going to say is going to cause problems for yourself and the people that you are speaking to.

Effective Communication Increases Your Confidence

Have you ever noticed how some of the most successful people in the world seem to ooze confidence? When they speak, the audience hangs onto their every word. That's because they're able to communicate well. When you can communicate effectively, your self-esteem and confidence level rise because you do not doubt at all that you can express and tell people exactly what you want them to know. When you can communicate well, you find that you are no longer shy and awkward when it comes time for you to speak, because you know exactly what to do and how to handle the situation.

Effective Communication Will Help You Go Far

Success cannot be achieved if you are not able to convey yourself properly. When people have a hard time understanding you, how will they be able to get along well with you? If you want to be successful at everything you do in life, you need to confidently be able to communicate effectively, because this is how you are going to set yourself apart from the rest. Do you notice how the most successful people in the world are the ones who can communicate effortlessly?

Mindset for Effective Communication

Before we begin our journey into critical conversations the first thing that we need to look at and master is our mindset. What most people don't know, realize or accept is that our mind is the most underused and most understood organ in the human body. With our minds we can accomplish anything that we can possibly imagine as well as limit ourselves to the most basic of tasks and possibilities.

When it comes to mindset it all comes down to what it is that you want and what you are willing to do or not do to achieve it. When looking at mindset, look at it as a coin. On one side we have everything that we want and desire whereas on the other side of the coin we have all of the excuses and issues that prevent us from achieving our goals. For the majority of us however we walk the edge of the coin looking down at the shiny side of our hopes and desires while favoring or listening to the doubts and echoes from the other side.

This is where the conversation starts. What side of the coin are you going to choose?

Your Self Image

The next layer of our mindset can be found in our self-image. The way that we look at ourselves and the way we perceive others looking at us is a major factor in our mindset and the actions that we engage. For instance, if you are someone who is overweight, doesn't speak well, has a disability or just doesn't feel right physically or emotionally your self-image will be affected by this. One the other side of the coin if you are slender, well educated, has a lot of friends and is healthier than ever your self-image will be greater resulting in more positive outcomes and conversations.

Knowing your abilities and limitations

The third level of mindset is our personal knowledge and understanding of our abilities and limitations. To stat this off I want to first say that no one is perfect. If you believe you are perfect, then you are living in a delusional world and are going to be in for a huge disappointment in life. However, if you know that you are not perfect and can accept that you have limitations then you have the foundation to build form and grow.

When we know and accept our limitations, we can better position ourselves into situations that we feel comfortable and in control. If we feel comfortable and in control, we are more likely to be in a better frame of mind to have more intelligent conversations with our inner voices. If, however, we find ourselves in situations that we are not comfortable in it is our job to restructure our mindsets to work in a positive way. And we can do this with critical conversations.

You are an island among many

The final component in regards to mindset is one that is seldom talked about or referred to. This is the knowledge that you are an island among many. What this basically means is that you are responsible for you first and foremost. Where many of us fall into the mindset trap is that we think of others first instead of ourselves. Now, I am not saying that you need to be selfish and self-centered. What I am saying is that at the end of the day when all of the kids are asleep, you are lying there in bed wide awake staring at the ceiling letting the events of the day fill your mind just know that you are one with yourself.

The actions that you perform or fail to perform will ultimately affect you in the end. Your kids will one day go off to school, your spouse may divorce you, you may lose or find another job, get a new house, car or win the lottery or eventually die. It is when we find ourselves in these situations we really begin to have these critical conversations with ourselves. Knowing how we plan to handle these conversations when they arrive will ultimately determine their outcomes.

Developing Assertiveness in Communication

One of the most vital skills to be an effective leader and communicator is developing assertiveness, which is starkly different from aggression. Assertiveness is standing up for yourself and not focusing on pleasing everyone all the time. This is done in a manner that is polite, firm, and non-offensive to others. Assertiveness is taking a balanced, reasonable, and win-win approach that considers the overall good. For instance, "I prefer going to a relaxed coffee shop rather than fine-dine restaurant" is a fairly assertive statement. It doesn't pronounce a judgment about what you want. It gives the other person an opportunity to give his/her view about it too. You are mentioning your preferences in a rational and balanced manner.

Assertiveness is clarifying your needs without using aggression or dominance. While aggressiveness involves disregard for another person's rights or needs, assertiveness is about putting across your needs in a polite, firm, and respectful manner. Unlike aggression that focuses on 'I win-you lose', assertiveness is about win-win. Take the aggressive version of the above-mentioned assertive statement. "We are going nowhere else but a relaxed cafe." This doesn't leave any scope for the other person to offer their views.

Assertive folks may not agree with a person. However, they will still respect the person's right to his opinion, beliefs, ideas, and preferences. They often respect the person's right to disagree. "We can agree to disagree" is a classic assertive statement. You don't give up your stand, and also respect the other person's right to stick to their stand. As an assertive person, you don't allow people to walk over you and know where to draw the line, while also respecting other people's values. Mutual respect and equality are the buzzwords of assertiveness.

Here are a few strategies to be a more assertive communicator:

One secret tip for building greater assertiveness is practicing in front of a mirror. Pretend that your boss, employee, team member, partner, or friend is standing opposite you. Have a mock interaction with them, where there are getting you to do something you don't to do. How best can you communicate this in an open, polite, firm, genuine, and non-offensive manner? Concentrate on everything from your expressions to words to body language. Watch out for the tone of your voice. How do you emphasize certain words to sound more assertive? When do you pause to create the right effect of what you've just said? Practicing this for a while will help you convey your point in a polite and balanced way.

Use more than "I" statements to accept responsibility for your emotions, thoughts, ideas, and feeling. For instance, instead of "we should never go to that restaurant" say, "I think we should avoid going to that restaurant." It prevents you from appearing dictatorial or dogmatic. Again, if you feel upset about your partner not contributing towards the baby's care, you can say something like, "I feel really upset that I wake up several times in the night. I need your help in caring for the baby."

Always view other people as a force you are working or collaborating with instead of working against.

This is even truer in work settings. Some people are always operating with the mentality that someone has to lose if they have to win. This isn't a sign of assertiveness. In any conflict or tricky communication situation, view people as allies instead of nemesis and try to work out a win-win situation for everyone involved.

Assertive people are seldom ruled by their emotions. Even in the most stressful and tense situation, stay calm and composed. Maintain eye contact with the person and keep your body language relaxed. Keep your tone steady, balanced, and uniform. Your thoughts will automatically mirror your body language. When you keep your tone, posture, and words balanced, the subconscious mind invariably assumes a more confident, self-assured, and assertive stand during disagreements and discussions.

Learn to say no. When you are up for something, learn to say a firm and polite no. There is nothing wrong in turning down things that aren't in line with your own priorities, values, goals, ideals, and preferences. Avoid feeling guilty about refusing other people. Our own negative self-talk induces pangs of guilt within us.

For instance, try reframing your inner voice from "I am not a nice person because I don't loan a part of my salary to a co-worker" with "I deserve to remain financially sound and take measures to prevent risking my financial security."

Another brilliant way to develop a more assertive communication style is putting yourself in the place of a loved one. What if he or she were being put through the situation you find yourself in currently? Would you hesitate to take up for them? It is easier for us to take a stand for our loved ones than ourselves.

Consciously practice expressing your opinion, needs, beliefs, and preferences in an open and clear manner. Don't assume that others will automatically know how you are feeling. This is a major reason for conflicts in relationships. We often assume that people will understand our feelings and needs, and avoid expressing them openly. Being an assertive communicator entails staying genuine, respectful, open, and clear about your needs, opinion, and preferences.

Use the repeated assertion technique for developing greater assertiveness.

It prevents you from being manipulated through verbal traps, misplaced logic, and argument baiting while sticking firmly and politely to your stand. The keywords are "calm repetition." Stay focused on your point. Let's look at a conversation to understand this more effectively.

"I would love to show you our new range of products."

"No thanks, I am not in the least bit interested in them."

"I also have a fabulous offering running on them for the holiday season."

"That's lovely. However, I am still not interested in seeing them right now."

"Would you like to carry a brochure and think about them?"

"No, I am not interested in them right now. If I decide to purchase in the future, I'll get in touch with you."

You demonstrate a consistent stand throughout the conversation through repetition. Repetition is a powerful form of assertiveness. It tells the other person that you aren't about to budge despite their fancy manipulation and persuasion tactics.

At times, you'll need to use negative assertion in your words to take a more comfortable and balanced look at the negatives in your behavior. This also ends up lowering the critic's hostility. You should embrace your shortcomings and faults with feeling the need to apologize excessively for them. Instead, agree tentatively with the hostile or negative criticism by saying something such as "Yes, you're correct. I don't always actively listen to what you say."

Chapter 4: History of Persuasion

Persuasion has a long history, going back to when humans discovered how to use it to our advantage. Persuasion is defined as a type of behavior that is employed as a means to influence someone's way of thinking, beliefs, decisions, motivation, and behavior.

It can be subtle and undetectable, done covertly, or more obvious, such as a form of encouragement.

The reasons for persuasion vary and are commonly used for personal and/or financial gain. It's a method applied throughout history for political and social gain. One notable example is how the Greeks viewed forms of persuasion, as a way to measure the suitability of a politician or position of authority. The ability to persuade was valued highly, and those who were successful were regarded as worthy of election.

Aristotle, a Greek philosopher, regarded persuasion as an essential skill to acquire and develop for a variety of reasons. It can be argued that persuasion, if used in its most skillful form, can deflect many negative attributes and help someone gain favor, regardless of the circumstance. An example of this is a court case, where a defendant or their lawyer can argue their innocence by way of persuasion. Even where a defendant is believed to be guilty, persuasion can (and has), convince a judge or jury that evidence is circumstantial or that a witness's testimony is not credible. There is more to this method than simply convincing an individual or group of a certain belief or concept with a smooth presentation and convincing words; it includes a far more in-depth study and observation of the people who are to be persuaded. Many of these attributes are useful in winning an argument or a case, whether the person employing the persuasion techniques is correct or not. In some cases, it's not about right or wrong, but instead, a variance in opinions or beliefs where persuasion can go a long way to convince people to see the other side of the debate.

What Are The Different Types Of Persuasion?

Rhetoric is a powerful method of persuasion, which involves the careful study and observation of people, either in groups, as individuals or in society, to better understand how best to apply the "art" of persuasion. Observing people would entail many studies, including employing skilled writers, artists, and speakers with the expertise and talent to persuade. A modern example of this method can be seen in advertisements aimed at specific demographics to promote the sale of a product, or a political campaign targeting undecided voters, to sway their decision one way or another.

The goal is not only to get your attention but also to maintain it by "speaking" to you in a way that evokes an emotional response or action. This could result in an emotional plea to support one political party instead of others or to purchase a certain product or service because of a certain nostalgia or connection with family or co-workers.

The reasons for using persuasive techniques is not always secretive or malicious: it can be a good way to convince someone to reconsider making the wrong decision that could result in a detrimental outcome, or serve as a form of positive encouragement or reinforcement as a form of empowerment, such as "you can do it" and "what have you got to lose, come on!" When persuasion takes on a more direct tone, it may seem like a strong form of encouragement. While this may work for some people, it doesn't have the same impact on others. Some people thrive on overt persuasion and may otherwise not achieve a milestone or "go for it" without that persuasive push. On the other hand, some people prefer more autonomy and do not respond well. This is where covert or more subtle forms of persuasion can be useful in influencing them.

Recognizing the different signs of persuasion is key to knowing if someone is using these methods on you. It may not be as obvious as coaxing someone to change their mind or try something new. Some forms of persuasion may be subtle and difficult to detect initially.

Understanding the reasons behind persuasive techniques and the different purposes they serve can help determine if you may be on the receiving end and the reasons why.

Three Basic Forms Of Persuasion

There are three types of persuasion: ethos, logos, and pathos, according to Aristotle. Each method appeals to a different source and has its reason for use:

Ethos

Ethos is known as the persuasion using ethics or morality as a basis. In this method of persuasion, the speaker or individual applying this method is trustworthy, credible, and knowledgeable. In their speech or debate, a credible person will make use of their related expertise and knowledge to support their argument. This is done by citing relevant sources and using their credibility as an expert to persuade the listener of their legitimacy.

This method is regarded as respectful in that it doesn't intend to sway the listener for unethical gain or advantage.

The speaker's reputation and status carry a lot of weight in terms of credibility, though this can also be established by using carefully constructed arguments that show that they are ethical.

Logos

Logos is based primarily in logic, or the application of logic to reason with or persuade someone. This method involves using evidence and related studies to support an argument.

A clear, concise form doesn't convince someone based on pseudo-science or skewed facts, but rather, it appeals to people who are not easily persuaded unless facts and their related sources support the argument. The format of logos is usually presented in a clear, sometimes chronological and progressive manner to show how a subject or topic began as disputable, followed by studies and observation to gain factual information to support the argument.

Pathos

Pathos is a method of persuasion that uses the emotion of the recipient (the person being persuaded). This is one of the most powerful and frequently used methods of persuasion. Pathos appeals to an audience's emotions, including their passions, imagination, creativity, and sympathetic nature. While the aim of this method is similar to logos and ethos, pathos can become very deceptive is using a vulnerable person's or group's emotions to their advantage. This can be seen in high control groups, where the promise of making lots of money or reaping the rewards of following a set of rules or belief system. Emotional persuasion can also be powerful in helping the audience identify with the speaker and/or their supporters, by sharing personal experiences and anecdotes that can convince people they are sincere and genuine, or "just one of us." The danger with employing pathos is how it can be misused to take advantage of a vulnerable or gullible group of people who are looking for quick answers and solutions to their problems.

Chapter 5: Dark Persuasion Skills

When people attempt to give meaning to the concept of persuasion, their answers always come in different forms. While some may set their minds on the advertisements and commercials that are everywhere in modern society, urging one to patronize a certain product or service over another, others' minds fall back to the politicians that try to change the minds of voters just to get one more vote at the polls. Both examples are correct as they are messages aimed at changing the perception of the subject.

The point of diversion between normal persuasion and dark persuasion is that dark persuasion does not always have a moral justification. While a normal persuader may try to persuade someone for that person's own good, a dark persuader does so with motivations that aren't always good for the other person. They try to get a full grasp of understanding of the person they wish to persuade, and they take pains to do so because they know what the biggest motivation is.

While persuasion always has moral implications, a dark persuader does not concern themselves with these implications. In fact, they are aware of them but choose to place their eyes on their objective(s) instead.

Persuasion is a psychological phenomenon in the everyday life of a human being. It is either that you are the one trying to persuade someone else or you are being persuaded. What makes the difference between dark and normal is the motivation behind it. In mass media, politics, advertising and legal decisions, persuasion comes into play all the time. The outcome of practicing it in these fields is determined by ways of persuasion which will influence the subject of persuasion.

There are some obvious and very crucial differences between persuasion and other types of mind control such as brainwashing and hypnosis. While these two require that the subject should be isolated in order to change their minds and identity, persuasion does not also require isolation.

In order to get to the goal, manipulation is used on one person. Although persuasion can also be done on a single subject in order to get them to change their minds, there is also a possibility of using it on a large scale to change the minds of a whole group or even an entire society.

For this reason, persuasion be a more effective mind control technique and perhaps more dangerous because it can change the minds of many people at the same time instead of the mind of just one person at a time.

There are several people that make the mistake of thinking they have an immunity to the effects of persuasion because they are of the opinion that they will always be able to see every sales pitch that comes their way. They believe they will always be able to use logic to get a grasp of what is going on and then find a logical conclusion to it.

Thanks to the fact that people are not always going to fall for everything they hear if they use logic, this may be true. It is also possible to avoid persuasion because the argument does not augur well with the person's beliefs no matter the strength of the argument.

However, there are people who know how to use persuasive messages to encourage people to patronize the latest gadgets or products in the market. This act of persuasion is very subtle so the subject will not always identify it, so it is going to be quite hard for them to always be able to form an opinion about the information they are going to get.

Every time persuasion is mentioned, it is very likely that one thinks of it in a bad light. This is because they tend to automatically think of a conman or salesman who is always trying to get them to change their perspective and who will eventually push them until this change is achieved.

While dark persuasion is prominent in sales and conning practices, there are also ways that persuasion can be used for good, like in diplomatic relations between international bodies or in public service campaigns. The difference only lies in the way the process of persuasion is brought to play.

Dark Persuasion Techniques

When a person is willing to change the mind of their subject by persuading them to do something that is contrary to their initial state of mind, the persuader is going to have some well laid out techniques to help them achieve their goals.

Each day that passes, the target is going to face different types of persuasion. For food makers, their goal will be to get their target to try out their new recipes or have them stick to the old ones, while studios will flash their latest blockbuster movies on the faces of their targets.

Whatever the case may be or whatever product they are selling, their main aim is to make more sales and that is why they are trying to persuade you. They really couldn't care less about how this will impact you and this is the reason why they must be very careful and skilled in the art of subtle persuasion to ensure that they do not tip you off or get you agitated. Since there are also many other brands trying to persuade you, they must find a unique way to impress their views on you.

Due to the influence of persuasion on a wide range of people, the techniques used in it have been a subject of study for many years, dating back to ancient times. This is because influence is a very useful tool in the hands of a wide range of people.

Starting from the early 20th century, the formal study of these techniques began to grow. Remember that the goal of trying to persuade people is to push a persuasive argument on an audience and have them convinced. They will then internalize this message and adopt it as their new attitude or even way of life. For this reason, there is a great need to discover the most successful persuasion techniques.

There are three dark persuasion techniques that have proven to be of great value over the years. We shall discuss those three in this section.

Create a Need

This is one of the most fruitful ways of getting a person to change their point of view or way of life. The person that is trying to persuade a target will either create a need or capitalize on a need that the subject already has. If this is done in a proper way, it has the potential of appealing a great deal to the target.

What this means is that in order to be successful, the persuader must appeal to the needs that are of more importance to the target. This may be their need to fulfil their dreams or of boosting their self-esteem. It may also be their want for love, shelter or food.

This method will always work out well because there is no way the subject is not going to need any of these things, or in need of anything at all for that matter. Since there is no way the target isn't going to have dreams and aspirations, the persuader will only have to find ways to make the victim understand how they can easily help the victim achieve those dreams.

The persuader may also tell their target that the target will realize their dreams if they make certain alterations to their beliefs or perspective. Doing this, according to the persuader, will give the target a higher chance of achieving success.

For example, a young man that wants to get intimate with a lady may tell her that he will help her improve her grades and finally make her parents proud by getting an A, but only if she becomes friends with him. While this lady may think that she has finally found the redemption she needs, the truth is that the young man isn't very interested in how well she performs in school, her academics are only a bait for getting access to sex.

Appealing to Social Needs

The other technique that the persuader can use is identifying the target's social needs. While this may not yield as many results and the target's primary needs will, it is still an important tool in the hands of the persuader.

There are people who are naturally drawn to crowds and desire to be wanted. They always want to have certain items, not because they need them but because it comes with certain prestige that makes them feel as though they belong to a higher class.

The notion of appealing to the target's social needs is what is obtainable through many TV commercials where viewers are encouraged to buy a product so that they will not be "left behind." When they can identify and appeal to the social needs of the target, the result is they are able to reach a new area of the target's interest.

Making Use of Loaded Words and Images

When a person is trying to persuade someone else, they must be careful with their choice of words as words can make all the difference. While there are many ways to say a thing, one way of saying it may be more potent than the other.

When it has to do with persuasion, one of the most important things is knowing how to say the right thing at the right time. Words are always the most important tools in communication and knowing the right call-to-action words.

Dark persuasion is one of the most powerful concepts of dark psychology, but sadly it is always overlooked and underestimated. This may be because, unlike the other methods of mind control, persuasion leaves the target with a choice. In the other mind control methods, the target is forced into submission and sometimes this is done by putting them in isolation so that at the end, they do not have any say in the outcome of the process.

When it comes to persuasion, the chips are laid bare (although with an ulterior motive in dark persuasion) so that the target is left to make the decision that they think will suit them best.

Chapter 6: Psychology of Manipulation

Who Controls our Lives?

It's interesting to see that manipulation has been around for a long time, and that is not a new or imaginary concept. Understanding what the art of persuasion is really all about is vital, to help you to deal with it.

In this chapter, we will look briefly at the psychology of manipulation. This allows us to see where it might occur in our lives. It will also help you in identifying those who might attempt to manipulate you. It is not only about people who like to dominate. If we don't know it is happening to us, might be encouraged to act in ways that are incongruous to our normal personality and behavior. Learn how commerce can persuade customers into buying their goods and services. Recognizing such methods will help in dealing with the power of persuasion.

We like to believe that we are individuals who make sensible choices. In our personal journey of life, we do not always have full control, and we don't always realize this. As children, we are influenced by our parents and have little control over how we raised. Once in the education system, we are further manipulated. The teachers will tell us all about the social norms and what is expected of us in society. As adults, we are lured in by politicians trying to get their share of votes. Many are persuaded to vote for a party because of what they promise for the future, even if they don't necessarily believe in their policies. This gives such politicians power, and their decisions will affect our lives. Are we really in control of our lives, or are we merely influenced by those who know all the tricks of persuasion?

Later in this book, we will look at how to deal with various manipulative methods, even sometimes covert. First, you need to learn to recognize when you are being manipulated so you can counteract it. For this purpose, we will now look at what the experts say on how this sort of behavior can exist among us.

Six Theories on Psychological Manipulation

1 Cognitive

There are many well recognized psychological processes in theories regarding the art of persuasion. One of those is the Cognitive Response model, developed by Anthony Greenwald in 1968. It is still relevant today for determining some factors in persuasion. It is also a model used extensively in the world of advertising.

Greenwald suggested that:

It is not the words of the message that determines the success of persuasion, but more the emotions of the receiver. The internal monologue of the one receiving the message will be deciding factor on how easy they are influenced. (2a)

Such internal thoughts will include positive and negative aspects, according to the individual's own personality. This not a learning process, but more based on whether the person already views the message with favorable or unfavorable thought processes (cognitions).

Overcoming any counter-arguments will rely on the expertise of the persuader.

They should stop their target from having sufficient time to construct any counter-arguments. The persuader must encourage positive arguments to come to the forefront. This gives the "persuasion effect" a better chance of success.

Persuasion can be more difficult if the intended target has been forewarned. It allows the target time to build their own counter-arguments, if the "message" is counter-intuitive to their present cognitions. The importance in pre-warning can be seen in research conducted by Richard E. Petty, in 1977. The study showed that students given notice about a certain event were less likely to be persuaded that those who had no pre-warning. (2b)

2 Reciprocity

Another well-studied explanation for how we might be open to the power of persuasion is the Rule of Reciprocity. This is based on a principle related to social conventions. If someone does you a favor, or does something good for you, then you are more likely to feel obliged to return the favor.

The Rule of Reciprocity can also happen subconsciously. Without even realizing it, you may agree to an action or favor asked of you by the requester. All because at some point they had done something for you, and you feel in their debt. You may feel obliged even if the request is something you would normally decline.

It is an effect widely used by companies who are looking to make sales. Often companies give out free samples, or time-limited trials. This is not without a motive. It is in the hope that the customer feels obliged to return the favor, and buy the product or continue with the agreement.

Reciprocity is a recognized psychological process. It is an adaptive behavior which would have increased our chances of survival in the past. By helping others, it is likely that at some later point they will help you. Though, it can also have negative effects. If someone does something bad to you, then you may be driven by the rules of reciprocity to exact your revenge.

The Rule of Reciprocity is well supported by academic research. Burger et al (2009), suggested that a group of participants were more likely to agree to a request if the requester had previously done them a favor. (2c)

3 Information Manipulation

A powerful tool in the manipulator's armory. This is a method of being outright deceitful. It is a means of providing limited and confusing information to the victim. The effect of this will unbalance their way of thinking, making them vulnerable. It can also incorporate the use of intentional body language, to persuade and manipulate someone.

A study by McCornack et al. (1992) (2d) showed the different ways a message can be falsified to assist in the manipulation process. McCornack's theory has a premise of four maxims, in a truthful statement. A breach of any of these will render the message as intentionally deceitful. The four maxims are:

Quantity

This is the "amount" of information provided. Most of us seek to provide the right amount of information so that the receiver understands our message. Not too little, or too much, as that might confuse. A manipulator though would play with that quantity of information. They may omit certain pieces they consider irrelevant. Most especially if it is likely to work against their argument. This is known as "lying by omission."

Quality

Refers to the "accuracy" of the information provided. Truthful communication is one of High Quality. If we were to violate this maxim, then the receiver hears intentional mistruths. This is "outright lying," to gain the manipulator power.

Relation

Here, we talk about the "relevance" of the information to the message. To confuse or sidestep an awkward question, the manipulator may go off topic. This is a way of changing the subject, for the sole purpose of misleading. It could be to hide their own weaknesses. Or even to over-emphasize on something that will give them more power over their listener.

Manner

The "presentation" of the message. An important aspect of this is body language. We read inflections and facial expressions as we listen. A manipulator may exaggerate these to mislead the presentation of the message. This is all in the aim to emphasize their own agenda.

Lying to manipulate or persuade someone is not a new concept. It is though, a method that is becoming particularly potent in the modern world. Online communication and social media do not always involve face-to-face contact. This makes it easier to tell mistruths or exaggerate information. A manipulator may in their elements with such communications.

4 Nudge

Not all manipulation is sinister. Sometimes we may be manipulated to help us make the right decisions for our own good. To do this, the Nudge Theory is particularly useful. The Nudge Theory expands positive reinforcement, by using small nudges.

Skinner's studies or behaviorism, show how useful this theory can be. (2a) With positive reinforcement, such as rewards, it can manipulate people into behaving in the manner that you are hoping to encourage.

One example of "nudging" can be seen in this example. Adding exceptionally high priced items on a menu may seem counterproductive.

Yet, the result of this actually increased the sales of the second highest priced item. The customers were given a "nudge" in the right direction, but for the benefit of the restauranteur.

Richard Thaler, considered the father of the Nudge Theory, was awarded the Nobel Memorial Prize in Economic Sciences. (2f) His contribution to behavioral economics was considered quite momentous. Nudge Theory gives positive reinforcement, or as Thaler described it, it gives "nudges."

The Nudge Theory is not only effective in economics. It can be used to encourage behavioral changes and influencing personal choices. Even accepted social norms can be manipulated to changes, in this way.

Nudging is so successful, that in 2010, the British Government set up a Department Behavioral Insights Team. This was to help develop policies. The department was referred to as the Nudge Unit.

There can be obvious benefits of using "nudges" to influence people. It is still a form of psychological manipulation that can infringe on an individual's civil liberties.

5 Social Manipulation

This type of manipulation is also known as psychological manipulation. It is often a tool for politicians, or other groups of powerful people who are used to advancing their own interests. In its worst form, it is a means of social control. By taking away individuality, it coerces the populace into accepting what is given to them. Though it can have a positive side when used to help with personal issues, such as improving health and wellbeing.

Those in power who use social manipulation may use distractive techniques to deflect from important issues. They would argue that their proposals are for the benefit of the populace, and the benefit of your family and its future. Anything you think personally, that might be different, is wrong and selfish. This type of persuasion is very paternalistic, almost treating individuals as if they were all children. This "system" will strive to make the crowds believe the things that have gone wrong are, in fact, their own fault. The only way to resolve the problem is to listen to the guidance of those who know better.

Such a political strategy would bring to forefront one social problem, only to hide another. It is a tactic to cause social unrest and panic among the populace. By creating unease in society, the populace will begin to demand changes. An example could be that the department wishes to hide the problems health care. So, they decrease the budget in crime prevention, causing crime statistics to rocket. The populace will receive information to coerce them into believing the best way forward for the crime problem. The politicians will feed propaganda, by disseminating their own truths and facts. It may not always be true, or it may be information that is exaggerated, such as misuse of statistics. This type of social manipulation could take years to get the end result that the manipulator requires.

The use of psychological manipulation is all a part of social influence. Professor Preston Ni, Communication Studies, published an article in Psychology Today. He indicates that one party recognizes another's weaknesses. They deliberately set out to cause an imbalance of power. This enables them to exploit their victims, for their own agenda. (2g)

Does this make us all social puppets? To some degree, it does. Most of us comply and conform to what is expected of us to avoid a society of chaos.

Think for a moment, what is the latest gadget or home improvement product that you would like to buy? Is it something a friend told you about, or a neighbor owns? Chances are it is something that someone else has, or you've read that it's popular on the internet, and that makes you desire it. This is another side of social manipulation. We can be so easily swayed if we let our guard down. Whether that is a good or bad thing, depends on how you personally view it.

As mentioned earlier, not all social manipulation is a bad thing. it can have positive aspects. The word "manipulation" might conjure up thoughts of a villainous individual/s bending you to their will. But, used correctly, social manipulation can help the populace, as a whole. Good examples of social manipulation are the "5 a day campaigns." Health specialists attempt to convince us to eat more fruit and vegetables. Or even the "stop smoking campaigns," which have resulted in reduced numbers of smokers.

The result of which is a reduction in smoking-related diseases. This is coercion at its best.

6 Gaslighting

This is perhaps the cruelest form of manipulation. It is a means of casting into doubt on the sanity and self-esteem of a person. You could say it is sowing the seeds of doubt into the victim of manipulation. Working on a similar principle such as "knowing you are being told repeated lies." Until eventually you begin to believe the lies as the truth.

It is an unkind form of manipulation. The gas-lighter will cause their victim to lose all confidence in their own credibility. This leads to completely destroying their own self-worth. All because they begin to doubt themselves. That is the intention of gaslighting, to reduce the victim to a psychological mess. The manipulator will constantly put their target down by contradicting them. Also by convincing them that they are always wrong. Sometimes to the point that the victim will be accused of telling lies. This is why the victim loses all self-esteem. When that happens, they become ruled by the domineering influencer. It is a form of mental abuse, often seen in abusive personal relationships.

The influencer will use constant techniques to make their victim doubt themselves. Even to the point of doubting their own memories, by denying things they've said and done.

Gaslighting takes a while before it is fully effective. The manipulator will wear his/her victim down over a long period of time. This type of manipulation is so insidious that it can eventually lead to the victim doubting their own sanity.

Dr. George Simon PhD is a Clinical Psychologist at a Texas university. He has studied people with disturbing personalities. The results of his studies caused him to believe that certain types of personalities, particularly psychopaths, are very adept at manipulation. They will distort the truth and use aggressive language, to set the wheels of doubt in motion in their victim's thoughts. Eventually, the target will lose confidence in their own judgment. They may feel shame and they will come to believe that the manipulator is right. This puts the target under the manipulator's control. (2h)

Gaslighting is not only restricted to individuals acting on one other.

It can be argued that it also has political uses. Columnist and author Maureen Dowd is one to follow this belief.

She argued that Clinton's administration used gas lighting techniques against a political opponent. Newt Gingrich, a member of the opposing political party, was often goaded into appearing hysterical. Some journalists and psychologists argue that Donald Trump also used gas-lighting techniques. Not only during his presidential campaign but also whilst in office. They argue he frequently says one thing, then denies he ever said it, which is classic gas-lighting.

Chapter 7: Covert Emotional Manipulation techniques

Even those who have a higher amount of emotional intelligence are going to be taken advantage of through their emotions. If they are not careful, a manipulator can step in and cause these issues, without any notice. Of course, the manipulator will often go for the easiest target that will give them what they want, and so, this drives them towards those who are lacking in healthy emotional activity. Those who struggle to keep their emotions in check are the ones who are most likely to run into trouble.

The manipulator is likely to mess with any of the emotions that they can. But there are three emotions that they like to prey on the most. These help them to guide you to how you should behave around this person in the future. You may not even realize the changes that are going on, which can make it that much harder for you to fight against the problem that is about to happen. Let's take a look at the three emotions that you need to be careful about, and explore how each one is going to be influenced and how you can protect yourself against these as well.

Happiness

Happiness is an emotion that a manipulator is going to want to work against you with. The resulting emotional state that you experience following the intense idealization phase of the manipulator is often going to include a lot of contentment and a feeling of being generally happy most of the time. You and the other person are getting along, and the relationship seems to be mutually beneficial for both parties. But to the manipulator, this is a concept that is meaningless and futile. They want to lure you here to have something to hold onto later when they try to direct some of your feelings the way that they would like.

This happiness is there on purpose. It allows the manipulator to build up a bond with you. They want you to feel some bond and some connection to them, but keeping you in this emotional state, and allowing you to remain happy for a long period is often going to lack a lot of the excitement and drama that they crave the most.

As time goes on, and you spend more time with the manipulator, you will find that they get frustrated and bored by the happiness that is there. It serves as their reminder that they need to take hold of the strings of your emotions and change your state into one that will help to feed their ego. They aren't going to be too concerned about how this is going to affect you. Instead, they are looking at the best way that this can benefit them along the way.

The manipulator will decide when you are allowed to be happy around them. They won't allow this emotion to come out just because they love you or care about you or anything like that. They will do it when they think the connection between the two of you is fraying and they need to make it strong again. Otherwise, your emotions will be toyed with until they can get what they want out of the situation.

Jealousy

The next emotion that your manipulator may try to work on with you is jealousy. They like to mess with this emotion because it can feed their egos, and helps them to get some more drama in their lives, which is something that they crave.

To do this, they will create their emotional state of jealousy using any manipulative tactic they can use as triangulation. Creating artificial rivalries that are not there, between you, their former exes, and any other party they can convince you are in the picture now.

This is going to serve the manipulator in several ways, especially if they are in a relationship with their victim, and they want that victim to feel like they are missing out or going to lose the manipulator. This ends up serving the manipulator in many ways.

First, it benefits the manipulator by keeping that ego as inflated as possible, which is super important to them. Second, it is going to ensure that the victim is focused on the manipulator's needs at all times in the hopes of holding onto the affection that the victim craves so much. And third, if the victim starts to increase their desperation to keep the attention of the manipulator, then it is going to give the manipulator a chance to label their victim as paranoid or crazy, and they can accuse the victim of over-reacting to the situation.

The main point of using this emotion and making their victim feel jealous which can be a super lonely experience to go through is that the manipulator wants to use this unstable emotional state to discredit the reputation of their victim. And often, it helps to make the manipulator look like they are the victim to those on the outside. This allows the manipulator not only to get some attention from the victim but also to get sympathy from those who are on the outside as well.

Anger

And the third emotion that we are going to focus on when it comes to dealing with the manipulator and how they treat their victim and how they try to control emotions includes anger. Anger is a powerful emotion, one that is hard to keep in check and control when you are handling it on your own. When there is someone on the other side, someone you thought you were close to, fanning the flames as well, then this makes things a little bit more difficult in the process as well.

Anger is going to follow often the manufactured feelings of jealousy that the victim is feeling. The manipulator can then use this to devalue the victim even more than before. There are a few methods that the manipulator can use to respond to the anger they are seeing from their victims.

First, the manipulator may choose to stonewall their victim, or become silent, and not give off any verbal response. They could even add in some frustration to the mix with a combination of projection, counter-accusations, and even something known as circular conversations or word salad. While the victim is justified with the anger that they have in this situation, the manipulator is going to be able to come out with a pre-made excuse to initiate a period of silent treatment. And then, after that period of the silent treatment, they can defend their decision by saying how necessary it was to escape the behavior of their victim.

The manipulator is often going to invoke pity from the victim, which is going to lead to some feelings of guilt, and of remorse. This is done because the manipulator would like their victim to take responsibility for the confrontation, and all of the things that have happened in that time, even though it was not the fault of the victim at all. Outward expressions of anger are going to be suppressed because the victim doesn't want to be irrational, and they don't want to bring about the silent treatment against themselves again.

As you can see, it is pretty easy for a manipulator to come in and take control over your behavior, by watching your emotional state and then trying to manipulate it to the best of their ability. You are going to crave the emotional stability and the happiness that come with the idealization phase, and this keeps you invested with the manipulator. They are going to grow fewer and further in between, but it is often enough to keep you interested and to stay.

A good manipulator can do a good balance here. They will bring up just enough of the happy and good times that you will remember them and want to stay. But for the most part, they are going to mess with your emotions, making you feel angry, crazy, and jealous all at once. This can make it hard to regain the control that you want over your life because you are too busy trying to figure out your emotions and what is going on. And when this happens, the manipulator has you right where they want you to be.

Ways that manipulators use emotions for their advantage

There are a lot of ways a manipulator can come onto the scene and cause issues. And the more they are allowed to mess with your emotions, the more trouble they can cause. Some of the things that they can do to mess with your emotional intelligence, no matter how high it may be, includes:

They play on fear. A manipulator is often going to exaggerate a lot of the facts that they have at their disposal, and they are going to feel just fine in overemphasizing specific points.

The next issue is that the manipulator is going to try and deceive their victim. All of us like it when we know someone else is being honest and transparent. But when it comes to a manipulator, they are going to try and hide the truth, or work hard only to show you the one side of the story that pushes you to act the way they want. For example, let's say that a manager at work tries to spread rumors that are unconfirmed about you in the hopes of gaining a strategic advantage in the workplace.

When this starts to happen, it may feel like there is nothing that you can do to make things easier. But the best step is never to believe all of the things that you hear. Rather than doing this, you could try and base your decision on a reputable source and make sure that you aren't afraid to ask questions when you feel the details are not as clear as you would like.

Many times, a manipulator is going to look at your emotions. And when they see that you are happy, they will try to take advantage of that. Often, when we are in a good mood, we are tempted to say yes to what others are asking of us. Or, we will see that there is an opportunity that looks good, and we want to jump at it, without getting a chance to think it through. The manipulator in your life is going to know about these tendencies and will use them against you.

The best way to take care of this problem and never get trapped because you were in a good mood is to learn to be more aware of all your emotions, and not just the negative ones. When it comes to making crucial decisions in your life, it is essential for you to achieve a good amount of balance in the process as well.

The manipulator is going to take advantage of the idea of reciprocity. These people know that it is so much harder for you to say no to them if they have already done some favor for you. This means that they are going to say yes to helping you with a small favor, will butter you up, and work to flatter you as much as possible.

When this happens, then they will ask you for a big favor. For most people, this makes it hard to say no to the other person. In order to avoid falling into this trap, it is important to have a firm grasp on your limitations. Learn that it is just fine to say no to helping someone else if you don't have the time, or in other situations where it is appropriate.

The next thing that you may see with a manipulator is that they like to push for what they consider the home court advantage. They will try to interact with you in a physical space where they are in control. This could be in their home, in their office, or in another place that they are familiar with, and you are not.

If it is necessary for you to negotiate with the other person, then it is best to do so in a space that is as neutral as possible. If you do need to meet the person on what is considered their home turf, then consider asking for some water and go with some small talk until you can get your bearings and get more comfortable in the unfamiliar location.

You may also notice that they are going to ask a lot of questions. Manipulators know that it is easy for the victim to talk about themselves. This is something that manipulators are going to take advantage of regularly and often, they are going to ask lots of probing questions with a hidden agenda behind them. Rather than being curious and wanting to know more about you, they are asking these questions to discover what weaknesses you have, and what information they can use later to their advantage.

Of course, just because someone is asking you questions and showing an interest in your life doesn't mean that they are trying to manipulate you. But be aware of the people who seem only to want to ask a ton of questions, and who are not willing to reveal the same kind of information about themselves at the same time.

You may notice that those who are looking to manipulate you are going to speak quickly.

This may be at a faster pace, or they are going to use special vocabulary and jargon to gain a good advantage over other people. If you feel like someone is talking too fast and you are not able to keep up, then ask if they can repeat their point, or ask some questions to see if they will clarify. If they get upset about this one, then it is a sign that you are dealing with someone who may not have your best interests at heart.

Manipulators are often going to display a lot of negative emotions. Some people are going to naturally use stronger body language or raise their voices to show that they are upset. This is often done to manipulate your emotions and make you feel like you are less than them. The stronger this emotion is, the more successful the manipulator is going to become because they will be able to convince you that you don't know what is going on, or that they are more important than you.

The best thing that you can do with this one is practice what is known as the pause. If you see that the other person you are talking to is demonstrating some strong emotions, take a moment rather than reacting right away. Depending on who the other person is, and the situation you are in, it is possible to walk away for a few minutes and feel better too.

You will also notice that a manipulator is going to be experts at putting the pressure on. They like to tell you about a good deal or something that you can't miss out on, and then they limit the amount of time given to you to react to the situation. They may try to take you by surprise and force you to decide within an unreasonable amount of time. The reason why they do this is that they want to coerce you into deciding before you have time to think it through and determine if it is the best course of action for your needs.

Remember that you are the one in charge, and you do not need to submit yourself to unreasonable demands. If your partner doesn't want to give you some more time to think things through, then it is better to step back. There is probably something wrong with the deal, and you don't want to end up dealing with that in the process either.

And finally, manipulators are good at giving you the silent treatment. When they try to deliberately respond to your reasonable calls, emails, text messages, and any other reasonable inquiry, the manipulator is taking all of the power and is making you wait. They want to make sure that there are some uncertainty and doubt in your mind. The silent treatment is going to be a head game, and the silence is the leverage that the manipulator is going to work with.

After you have been able to attempt communication to a reasonable degree, such as texting a few times or sending an email, it is time to set the deadline. This lets them know that you are not going to hold out forever and let them play with you. In situations where there are no other alternatives than working with this person, you may need to have a frank discussion that helps to address the communication style of the other person as well.

There are always going to be those people who will work to increase their emotional awareness, both in others and in themselves. And sometimes, these individuals are going to use that power to manipulate and influence others. And this is something that you need to use to help sharpen your emotional intelligence. This ensures that you are as protected as possible when the other person tries to use things against you.

Chapter 8: Deception

Understanding what gives deception away is an essential part of learning how to become a good liar. You can lie through your teeth, but it will create more harm than good if you don't know how to avoid detection. A good liar is able to act natural, but he is also prepared. He knows what to say and do when people try to detect his dishonesty. A good liar is also wise about lying. He thinks, why lie when he doesn't have to? Lying takes a lot of effort. He knows that if he conserves that energy for when he really needs it, he will be a better liar on the rare occasions when he lies. He also knows that he will earn an honest reputation and won't earn the mistrust of others.

So here are some tips on how to become such a good liar that you could even fool an FBI interrogator, who is an expert at catching liars.

Have a Reason

Lying all the time is no way to become a good liar. Sure, practice makes perfect, but when you lie a lot, you run the risk of getting sloppy. You damage your honest reputation. If you are a known liar, no one will believe you. You're more likely to get caught in lies in the future if people suspect that you lie about everything. It is far better to have an honest reputation, where people think that you a good person who never lies. Then people won't have as much reason to suspect you of dishonesty.

Of course, this means that you should be honest more than you should be dishonest. Save the lying for when you really need to lie. Basically, only lie when you have a good reason to.

Weigh each situation in your head. What would the consequences of the truth be? You might make someone unhappy with the truth, but will that unhappiness go away? Is this something that other people can get over? Or will it ruin your reputation, your friendships, and more? If you have a lot to lose by telling the truth, still consider telling the truth. People will often forgive you for the truth. Lying makes things ten times worse. But if you absolutely cannot tell the truth, then you can consider lying.

The more you need to lie, the more likely you are to pull it off. You stand to lose a lot and you have great motivation for lying. Therefore, you will do your best to tell a convincing lie.

Rehearse

Before you lie, it is best to organize your mind. Get things right so that when you tell your tale, you won't mess up.

First, determine your target. Who are you lying to and why? What story will make the most sense to this person and minimize your risk of getting caught? Know who you will be lying to in order to design the best lie possible.

Second, think up a logical story. Fill in all gaps. Come up with lots of details to make your story believable. Think of questions or problems that others may bring up and come up with explanations. You may have to think fast but don't let that get you nervous. This is a chance to be very creative.

Next, practice your lie in your head so that you memorize it. That way, when you're on the spot being interrogated, you are prepared with what to say. You won't spend as much time scrambling to make up details on the spot and creating an incoherent story that gives away your deception.

Watch Your Tenses

Liars tend to mess up the tenses of their sentences when they are fabricating part of a story. When someone is reviewing true events that occurred in the past, they will naturally use the past tense. When they switch to a fabrication, their brain suddenly is in the present, trying to invent a story on the spot. Thus, they start using the present tense.

Watching out for rapid and unexplained tense switches or jumps in conversation is a great way to spot if someone is being less than truthful. But you can also use this knowledge for your own excellent lying. Avoid detection by rehearsing your story beforehand and being careful to maintain the same tense.

Tell the Truth as much as Possible

Another great secret to lying well is to tell the truth...in a misleading way. The more truth that is in your lie, the easier it is for others to verify. You look more honest this way. You also can blame lapses in truth on faulty memory, should anyone find out about the bit of falsehood that you snuck in with the truth.

Lying by Omission

Lying by omission is one way to do this. You tell the truth, but leave out one key detail. However, you want to make sure that this detail is totally obscured. People know all about lying by omission. They will watch you for this. You need to have a good cover for the event that someone spots your omission.

When you omit part of a story, make sure that there are no obvious holes. You want to make sure that the story connects. So when you leave something out, the story overall is still cohesive. You can make up a few details to bridge the gap.

Deliberate Misleading

How you word things is also a great way to mislead people without outright lying.

You can use certain phrasing that leads people to draw wrong conclusions on their own. If they ever find out the truth and confront you for lying, you can say, "But I told you the truth!" Really, you did.

Deliberate misleading is a pretty advanced technique. Learning how to use language to purposefully mislead someone without getting caught is an art. But that's why you've graduated to Dark Psychology 202, right?

The art of misleading requires you to make others draw incorrect conclusions on their own. Offering just a few certain words can make someone believe something that you are not really saying. People tend to draw ideas from their own biases. Knowing someone's bias helps you figure out what conclusions they are likely to draw based on the language you use.

Here are a few examples that can show how misleading works. From there, you can build your own misleading tales when you need to.

Someone asks you if a girl is your girlfriend. You like her so you don't want him to hit on her, but meanwhile she isn't yours. Instead of telling a direct lie that she is your girlfriend, you can just say, "We talk." That's so vague, but it means different things to different people.

This guy will probably infer from it that you two have something going on.

Your mother wants to know where you have been. You can tell her that you went to a friend's house and then start talking about how your best friend Mark's sister kept saying something funny. She will infer from this that you were probably at Mark's house. In reality, you never told her whose house you were at.

Your boss asks why a project isn't moving forward. You honestly haven't had time to get it done, but you don't want to lose your job. So you say, "Events have transpired that making moving forward difficult but I'm on it." Your boss may guess that the events you speak of are hurdles that you encountered with the project. He won't guess that really these events are just personal events that have prevented you from dedicating your full time to this project.

True Details in a Lie

When you lie, you can still include bits and pieces of the truth. Pepper your lie with truthful details as much as possible. The more truthful details you can include in your story, the better. You want to avoid fabricating as much as possible. This is good for two reasons: the first reason is that the fewer untruths you make up, the less you have to remember.

Making things up takes some energy and effort, so it's best to conserve that energy as much as possible. The second reason is that truthful details are verifiable. That makes it seem like you are telling the truth and nothing but the truth.

You can tell someone that you were at a friend's house. Then provide some real details about the house and the party that you heard through a friend. This makes it seem like you were actually there.

False Confession

Admitting to something embarrassing or revealing a secret can help confirm your innocence. You want to distract people and convince them of your innocence by claiming that you were doing something embarrassing and personal. You also build trust and create a false bond when you tell someone a secret.

Let's say you were in the wrong place at the wrong time. You don't want to admit to what you were really doing, so you make up something else nefarious that is a little less terrible than what you were actually doing.

So you could say, "I was seeing my mistress" or "I was at the porn shop." This embarrassing confession both explains why you were where you were and it makes others uncomfortable. They are less likely to press the line of questioning. They will also think that you are telling the truth, since the truth must have been hard for you to admit.

Posture and Eye Contact

Your physical moves are what usually give away your deception. Lying takes a lot of mental energy and emotional discomfort. This manifests in your eye contact, gestures, and movements. Physical clues that give away the fact that you are lying are usually called "tells." Everyone has a tell. But if you want to avoid detection, you must never reveal your tell.

First, let's look at some of the common ways that liars act when they're trying to deceive someone.

- Grooming: Excessive grooming indicates that a liar feels dirty or bad subconsciously. He makes up for this by grooming his facial hair, straightening his tie or clothes, cleaning his nails, or otherwise performing grooming gestures while talking.

- Organizing. Much like grooming, a liar feels disorganized when he lies. He attempts to make up for this by organizing the environment around him. He might straighten papers on the desk in front of him, for instance.

- Lack of Eye Contact. A liar who is afraid of giving away his deception won't want to make direct eye contact. He will look anywhere but into your eyes. He may become overly focused on a point in the distance to allow him to stall as he thinks of a story, or he may look to his right as he uses his imagination to come up with something.

- Too Much Eye Contact. The reverse of this is the liar who makes too much eye contact to convince someone of his honesty. Too much or too little eye contact is never good. Try to make a normal amount.

- Stuttering. As he stalls for time to think of a lie, he will stutter and use lots of meaningless filler words. He might even mumble, so that it's impossible to understand what he says. There are just his ways of stalling for time and making it difficult to hear what he has to say.

- Fidgeting. Fidgeting denotes nervousness. A liar will fidget in his seat, pick at things, play with his hair, drum his fingers on the table, bite his lips, chew his nails, play with some small object like a paper clip, or some other nervous gesture. A good liar will be relaxed and calm.

Believe Your Own Lie

Why do people lie? Usually, people are inherently honest. But they will rapidly become dirty, rotten liars when they know that someone will disapprove of their actions. Keeping this in mind can help you become a better liar.

Consider how you want to please someone. Then create a reality that would please that person. Believe in that reality. Strive to please them. This will motivate you to not only lie, but to lie well.

The key to lying is to become comfortable with it. How can you do this? One way is to make yourself believe your own lie. This is the trick that pathological liars use. They literally create false realities in their minds to convince themselves that they aren't lying. Then they tell their false stories with conviction, as if their stories are real.

These ties into rehearsal. Rehearsing lies is essential to lying well. Rehearse your reality.

Avoid Common Phrases

A lot of people have common phrases that set off alarm bells. Learn these phrases so that you can avoid them. Here are some major ones.

"Why would I lie?" "Would I ever lie to you?" "Have I ever lied to you before?" These defensive phrases are telltale signs that someone is lying, so avoid using them. A liar wants to convince someone that he or she is being honest. An honest person doesn't have to do this. So don't dedicate too much time to convincing someone of your honesty. Rather, behave calmly, as if you are comfortable with the fact that you are telling the truth. People will be more likely to believe you. If you dedicate too much time to convincing someone that you are innocent, then you will provide a dead giveaway that you are lying.

Getting super defensive or indignant when people don't believe what you tell them is another form of subterfuge, where you are basically trying to distract from the lie. Don't get too defensive or people will see red flags. Instead, act like your honor is everything to you and you are committed to convincing this person. How would you feel if you were actually being honest?

Imagine that feeling and then channel it. Lying is a bit like acting. You want to act innocent and behave just as you would if you were being unfairly accused of lying. You might get adamant and emotional, but you're not going to act like you're offended. Convincing someone that you're not lying would be your priority as an honest person.

Don't Be Evasive

Liars are evasive of the truth. Therefore, they try to avoid answering questions. Their dodging of questions not only frustrated the person who is asking, but it gives away the fact that they are not comfortable with this conversation for some reason. Therefore, being direct makes you appear honest.

There are many forms of deceptive evasion. The most common is changing the subject. A liar will want to get off of the uncomfortable subject for fear of giving away the fact that he is being dishonest. As a result, he wants to switch topics as rapidly as possible. Beat the average liar's game by casually agreeing to remain on the subject. You don't need to keep talking about it, but as long as the other person wants to talk about it, you can keep providing details and answering questions.

A rapid subject change is always suspicious, so never does that.

Another form of evasion is being very vague. A liar will be vague to avoid giving away too many details. Details can get messy. But if you choose to be direct and provide lots of details, you appear honest. You set people at ease. Don't use vague language; stick to direct and clear terms. People will assume that a liar doesn't speak so directly and tacitly.

A common way that liars use vagueness is by using the passive tense. "The door got locked," is something a liar would say. But now that you know better, you would say, "I locked the door." Don't try to escape responsibility with passive language. Other people can see right through that ploy.

Liars will also use "softer" language to lessen the impact of what they did and ease the burden of their guilt. For instance, a liar might say, "The painting was taken," rather than "The painting was stolen." Stolen is a stronger word than taken so liars don't want to use it. However, you can stay a step ahead of most liars and use the proper terms for what you are talking about.

An evasive person will also try his very hardest to avoid talking about the situation that he is being dishonest about. He will do anything to dodge talking about it. Thus, he will try to evade answering questions by asking questions of his own, joking around, and otherwise trying to distract the interrogator. Distractions are one of the sneakiest forms of evasion. Staying on topic is a good way to establish the sense that you are telling the truth.

One way to spot a liar is when he or she tries a little too hard to be non-evasive and gets a little too involved. For instance, if there is an organizational investigation into a theft in the office, you can bet the person who screams the loudest about the theft is guilty. He or she thinks that by being very involved, he or she will seem innocent and will escape detection. But being too involved is very suspicious. You don't want to be evasive, but you don't want to be over-involved. Strike a rather neutral balance.

Chapter 9: Dark Psychology techniques and applications

Most psychological techniques have a dual purpose – they can be used for both dark psychology and white psychology. What differs is the intent of the person employing the techniques.

In this chapter, we will concern ourselves with psychological techniques employed to achieve nefarious intents.

Dark persuasion

Persuasion is by far the most employed psychological technique. Most of the time, it is used for White psychology. As a tool for White psychology, almost all of us have used it in one way or another. However, very few of us have employed persuasion as a dark psychology tool.

Before we venture into the depth of Dark persuasion, let's look at the crucial components of persuasion as a whole.

What is persuasion?

Persuasion is a psychological technique of presenting arguments in such a way that motivates, influences, or changes a person's attitude, or behavior in order to achieve the desired outcome.

Persuasion tips

The following are important tips you need to master in order to become successfully persuasive:

- Do your research – to gain knowledgeable authoritative
- Be a thought leader – to guide people in your thoughts
- Be confident
- Appeal to emotions

Use rhetoric statements and assertions

- Keep sarcasm to the minimum
- Sound reasonable
- Watch reactions
- Be subtle in responses
- Actively listen

- Suggest, don't demand

- Be actively observant

- Be emotionally intelligent

Persuasion tactics

The following are basic yet important persuasion tactics:

- Use the name of the person you are engaging with

- Make a personal connection

- Build rapport

- Create an opportunity for reciprocity

- Use motivating words

- Be dynamic and adaptive – like a chameleon, change to suit your target's uniqueness (no blanket approach). Use NLP's mirroring and matching technique.

- Take advantage of the Bandwagon effect

- Create some scarcity in the mind of the person you are persuading

- Inspire curiosity through deliberate information gap (suspense)

- Use a foot in the door tactic – make a small request that opens the door wider for an eventual big request

- Clearly, point out the benefit of your proposition to the person you are persuading. Remember everyone subconsciously asks, "what is in it for me?"

The Bandwagon effect

Bandwagon effect refers to that effect a crowd or group of people has on its constituent member.

The following are some characteristic attributes of the bandwagon effect:

- The herd mentality – people are persuaded to follow each other

- Social proof - people tend to follow the most popular cause of action. For example, decrying negative social proof (such as littering, logging, bad sexual behavior, bingeing, smoking, etc) may actually promote it.

  For example, in case of 20% absenteeism, instead of the manager decrying that there is an increase of absenteeism from the previous 15%

to now 20%, the manager should also reinforce positive social proof by pointing out to the majority who have remained not absent (i.e. 80%) and talk of the 20% as few spoilt apples that should be minimized.

Dupery

Dupery is an act of deception. However, dupery goes further too selfishly gain from the victim. In dupery, the manipulator sets traps or baits into which the victim falls in and then gets exploited for selfish or nefarious gains.

Indoctrination

Indoctrination is the act of imparting someone with a set of beliefs without offering that person an opportunity for critical inquiry.

Indoctrination strategies:

- Rote training – this is an act of enforcing information into people's memory through repetitive action. For example, uttering certain mantra during prayers, or counting mala beads while praying.

- Affirmation–making people say words that positively approve certain statements. This way, they are programmed to hold those statements as true.

- Obstruction of truth and facts–this is a deliberate action aimed at making those being indoctrinated not to access sources of truth or facts. For example, they can be barred from reading certain books that are deemed "satanic". Fear psychology is often employed, like telling people that they will have nightmares or be visited by vampire spirits in their sleep if they read such a book.

- Confession–everyone one of us has a "sinful" past. We all have skeletons in our past... things that we did and feel guilty about. One indoctrination strategy is to force people to confess. Once they confess, they lose the moral authority to stand upright before the indoctrinators. As such, they become more submissive toward indoctrination.

- Isolation – the main aim of isolation is to cut out someone from the influence that may make indoctrination impossible or difficult to achieve. Thus, the victims are cut off from the rest of the family, society or normal relationships.

Isolation is one form of obstruction of truth and facts since the victims cannot get a second opinion about assertions being made by the indoctrinators.

- Guilt imposition – guilt imposition is closely related to forced confession. However, in guilt imposition, a sense of guilt is postulated into the victim's mind. The victim may be unknowingly ensnared to commit a wrong and then indoctrinator finds ways to discover it. Later on, the indoctrinator uses that act to impose guilt on the victim. The primary objective, just as forced confession, is to lower the victim's moral standing and hence cower the victim into psychological submission.

- Phobia imposition – phobia is psychological fear. Indoctrinators induce phobia into their victims such that they find it hard to exist outside the indoctrinator's domain. For example, the victim can be told of how the 'devil' wants to kill him and the only way to salvation is to leave that devil-infested home and come to live with the indoctrinator who has the powers to chase away the devil. There are many forms of phobia imposition. For example, insurance companies impose phobia on their potential clients by exaggerating the potential risks that may happen should the potential client not insure the life of loved ones or property. Governments also prey on their citizens by instilling phobia, especially when they want their agenda to prevail.

- Rituals – rituals have a strong effect on one's psychology. This is why most traditions, religions, cults, political organizations, and even some civil organizations have rituals. For example, it is common for rituals to be performed prior to prayers, prior to burials, prior to the war, etc. Rituals enhance a person susceptibility to a certain proposition being advanced by the indoctrinator.

- Induced dependency – induced dependency is commonly applied by manipulators in a relationship where they want to gain an upper hand over their victims. For example, imperialist or colonialist entities can perpetuate poverty in their target society and then pretend to be saviors of that society. They may dish out conditional aid, conditional grant, etc… with the conditions carefully crafted to increase dependency and make the victims more susceptible to exploitation. Since, without this deliberate impoverishment, that particular society would not have become susceptibly poor or would not have welcomed the conditional aid and grant, this becomes and induced dependency. In marriage partners, it is common for an insecure partner to create a condition that makes the other partner dependent. For example, an insecure husband can push or trigger his wife to lose employment. Once the wife loses employment, then, the insecure husband feels comfortably in control of the unemployed wife since he is the main breadwinner. The wife's lack of financial independence makes her become more susceptible to the dictates of the husband.

- Punishment – by having a system of tests and exams and offering incentives for those who pass the indoctrination program

Characteristics of indoctrination

Unsurprisingly indoctrination takes place in most domains of our lives. It takes place in our homes (by parents), in schools (by teachers), in public life (by politicians and governments), etc.

The following are some of the key characteristics of tools used for indoctrination:

- Fear
- Dogmatism
- Fundamentalism
- Cognitive closure
- Feeling of inadequacy
- Perceived deprivation

Sources of indoctrination

While there are some covert sources of indoctrination, the following are some of the common overt sources of indoctrination:

- Religious institutions
- Schools and educational establishments
- Media – mainstream, alternative media, social media
- Parents
- Politicians
- Marriage partners

Brainwashing

Brainwashing refers to erasing from one's belief system the existing set of old beliefs and in its place supplanting a new set of beliefs. Brainwashing happens without someone's will.

While sometimes, brainwashing is subtle and involuntary, a lot of time it is violent. For example, we have had forced conversions during the crusade period and also during the jihad. In the forced conversion, the victims are fully aware that they are being brainwashed but accept it as a coping mechanism to avoid greater harm such as death.

Violent brainwashing happens most in the militant cultic or criminal organizations where victims are trapped and have no exit option.

Potential victims of violent brainwashing include:

- Prisoners (especially prisoners of war)
- Slaves under captivity
- Kidnapped victims
- Illegal aliens

In the subtle brainwashing, often the victim voluntarily and unknowingly accepts brainwashing. In this case, the perpetrator looks out for susceptible victims who are more malleable. The victims are often in a desperate situation and thus have a psychological void that desires fulfillment.

The following are some of the potential victims of unknowing brainwashing:

- Those suffering from unknown chronic illness
- Minors who have left their home to live alone and often faraway
- Those who have lost their jobs and are in deep despair
- Those who have lost their loved ones, especially through divorce or death

Common steps in brainwashing

The following are some of the common steps taken by brainwashers to brainwash their victims:

1. Isolation
2. Attack on self-esteem
3. Subjugation
4. Testing
5. Love bombing

Isolation

The brainwasher knows that a person's family or close circle can easily notice what is happening and thus rescue the victim. As such, the first step they take is to isolate the victim from close family and friends.

Some, like cultic leaders, can instill negativities about close family and friends. This brings division between the victim and loved ones and thus breeds psychological isolation. For example, a cultic leader can claim that your closest friend is a psychic vampire that drains your energy thus making you chronically ill and as such, you ought to keep off from that friend. Since you are sick and desperate, you are likely to follow this brainwashing tactic and thus find yourself isolated from the very person who could have saved you from brainwashing.

Attack on self-esteem

It is only a victim who has self-doubt, low self-confidence, and on the overall suffers from low self-esteem that can easily be brainwashed. As such, the brainwasher seeks to achieve this state in the victim by attacking the victim's self-esteem.

Some of the ways by which the brainwasher attacks the victim's self-esteem include:

- Verbal and physical abuse – this often applied in violent brainwashing where the brainwasher uses abuse as a means of demeaning the victim so that the victim loses self-worth.

- Sleep deprivation – a sleep-deprived person is more likely to submit to psychological pressure since there is lack of full consciousness. It is much easier for a sleep-deprived person to submit to brainwashing instructions just to have an opportunity to be left alone and sleep.

- Intimidation–Intimidation is one of the tactics employed by brainwashers to push someone into involuntary submission. For example, the threat of punishment is a form of intimidation.

- Embarrassment – this is used especially if the victim has some dark secret that he or she wouldn't like to be revealed. For example, a brainwasher may resort to using tricks to obtain nude photos of a potential victim or trick such a victim into marital infidelity. Once the brainwasher acquires these materials, he/she starts subtly embarrassing the victim. In this subtle embarrassment, the brainwasher doesn't reveal the materials to the public but uses generalized terms that insinuate immorality on the part of the victim. The victim knows where the cues are leading to and thus does everything possible to dissuade the brainwasher from revealing these embarrassing contents. Thus, the brainwasher attains an upper hand which he/she uses to brainwash the victim. For example, the victim could be forced into performing rituals that wear the victim's self-worth and self-esteem thus becoming deeply captive to the brainwasher. Eventually, the victim may be infected by the Stockholm syndrome, where, instead of acting against the brainwasher, acts to protect the brainwasher – an act, which, subconsciously is more about protecting the "secrets" (embarrassing content).

- Scarcity creation such as rationing of basic necessities and only released upon the victim's obedient performance.

Subjugation

Brainwashers seek to bring the victim under their absolute control so that the victims become absolutely obedient.

The following are some of the tactics used to achieve subjugation:

- Extreme abuse
- Us -vs- Them
- Love bombing

Extreme abuse

The victim is passed through extreme abuse. Almost often emotional and psychological abuses are employed. Physical abuse is only employed in violent brainwashing. Physical abuse is not employed in the subtle brainwashing.

Us -vs- Them

The victim is coerced to make a choice between the brainwasher and the rest of the world. However, the victim is not granted an exit option.

The victim is introduced to those who are already brainwashed and thus praise the brainwasher. In case the victim still thinks of "them" (the outside world) as an option, the victim continues to be subjected to extreme abuse until he or she comes the ultimate choice of belonging to "us", that is, joining the rest of the brainwashed subjects.

Testing

Testing happens to establish whether the victim has ultimately made the "us' choice and no longer desires to join "them". It is also done to test the victim's level of obedience.

Sometimes, under secret control, the victim may be released to "them" (the rest of the world) on the condition that he or she should return on a certain date. The victim is then secretly monitored to see whether he/she desires to return to "us" (the brainwashed group).

If the victim does not desire to return to "us", then, the victim is kidnapped and returned to the fold upon which the vicious cycle begins.

On the other hand, if the victim voluntarily returns to us, then, the victim is taken to the next stage, that is, love bombing.

More often than not, due to isolation and induced dependency, even if the victim desires to rejoin "them", the victim finds it such a long journey to recovery and hence prefers getting back to "us" rather than starting all over again to rebuild the lost life.

Love bombing

Once tests are done and prove that the victim has been effectively brainwashed, love bombing is applied to galvanize the victim into the fold.

Love bombing could be in the form of praising, promotion in the order of subjects, receiving gifts, etc.

Negative effects of Dark hypnotic induction

There are many victims of dark hypnotic induction. The following are some of the common causes of dark hypnotic induction:

- Being hypnotized to such an extent that you willfully give your possession to the hypnotist
- Being hypnotized such that you willfully open your door to robbers
- Being hypnotized such that you voluntarily follow kidnappers to their den.

Chapter 10: Dark seduction techniques

The first approach that we will look at is known as the indirect approach. One mistake that you may see in conventional dating is that one or both parties will offer an icebreaker, one that is usually unappealing and cheesy, when they try to introduce themselves to someone new. They may say something like "You look pretty," "Nice eyes," or "Good song, right?"

Why are these icebreakers so bad? It is likely that the victim of your seduction has heard these countless times, and as soon as they hear them, they will be turned off and not want to talk to you at all. When the seducer uses such a bad line, it often leaves the impression that they are unappealing and bland, and no one wants to waste their time on a relationship with that kind of person.

With the indirect opener, the seducer is throwing in a breath of fresh air compared to the opening lines we talked about before. An indirect opener is going to be an icebreaker that will start the social interaction but won't convey any sexual intent. Often it is going to be posed as an "intriguing question."

 A good example of this would be when the seducer asks something like "Settle this for me or my buddies over there – do men or women lie more?" This is a different way to open up and talk with the other person and can start up a new conversation. And it shows the victim that the seducer is very interesting and is interested in a good conversation.

These indirect openers have the advantage of eliminating the possibility of rejection. The person who uses this kind of opener is not really offering themselves to the victim of the seduction. It is basically impossible to reject something that wasn't even offered, so it takes that part out of the equation.

Another technique to use with dark seduction is social proof. People who are popular are going to be more attractive compared to those who aren't. It is a human instinct to assume that if another person is liked by a lot of people, then there must be something that makes that person likable.

Social proof is an example of showing is more powerful than telling. Many people will try to talk about their success or their popularity, but this isn't a good idea.

It is going to seem like you are bragging and can be a big turnoff to the other person. It is better to simply make sure that you are at a table or near others who are interesting. This is going to convey your social value, without seeming like you are showing off in the process.

Of course, social proof can be used for devious purposes. Think about a psychological seducer who is at a club or a bar. They see a girl that they want to seduce. Rather than directly approaching this person, they will decide to approach someone else and start a conversation with them, before moving over to their original target. This can remove the idea that the seducer is lonely, and it can sometimes spark a little jealousy that works in advantage to the seducer.

You can also work with a frame of leading to help with dark seduction. Many times you will find that the people you meet are happy to be led. Indecisiveness is one of the least attractive qualities in others.

If you are able to show that you are decisive, you can automatically get the attention of others.

There are several ways that the dark seducer can show their decisiveness and that they have the ability to lead. Some of these could be physically moving around a venue, making the suggestion that it is time to change venues and not being scared to disagree with what someone else has said. Many men try to be indecisive around their victim because they don't' want to come off as weak. This is going to work against them. A dark seducer knows that they need to be decisive if they want to have any chance with the other person.

In addition to some of the techniques that we have talked about above, there are some seducers who are able to harness some of the other dark psychology traits, such as the use of psychopathy, in order to reach their romantic goals. For example, one trademark of psychopathy is the ability of the seducer not to feel any fear when they interact with other people.

Many times a man or a woman is going to be paralyzed by fear, especially when there is a chance for rejection by someone they are interested in. A dark seducer is not going to have this fear because they just don't understand the fear at all. Even if you are not a dark manipulator and you don't regularly use dark seduction, you can use this idea.

A psychological seducer is going to learn, over time, that it is better to be the one who tried and failed rather than the one who didn't have any confidence to try in the first place.

Why Are Dark Seducers So Dangerous?

A dark seducer can be a formidable foe. They know exactly how to get the other person, their victim, to fall in love with them. But the problem comes with the fact that the dark seducer really isn't in love with the other person. There is something that the dark seducer wants out of the relationship. This could be companionship because they don't like to be alone, sex, or something else. But they are usually not looking for love at all.

As soon as the victim of this seduction doesn't provide the thing that their seducer wants, the seducer is going to leave. So, if the victim starts to feel that they are being used and withholds sex from the seducer, the seducer will simply leave the relationship and move on to their next victim.

The seducer has no worries about the other partner in the relationship. A true seducer is only going to see the other person as a tool, something that helps the seducer get the pleasure that they want.

As soon as that tool stops doing the job that it's supposed to, the seducer will move on to find a new person to do the work for them.

A dark seducer may move quickly between one relationship to the next, or they may even stay in a relationship for a long time. It all depends on the situation and how long the seducer is able to keep the victim under their control. Some victims stand up for themselves pretty quickly. The longer the victim is under the control of the dark seducer, the harder it is for them to leave.

This doesn't mean that the dark seducer has learned how to love their victim. It simply means that the dark seducer has become used to the way that things are, and they will use their powers and their mind control techniques in order to keep the victim right where they are.

How to Avoid Dark Seduction

It is important for you to be aware of dark seduction. While some men may choose to use some of the ideas of dark seduction in order to help them gain some confidence, avoid some issues with their fear of rejection, and make it easier for them to meet women, there are many that will use these techniques because they don't really care about the other person at all. They have specific goals that they want to reach in the relationship, and they will get there, no matter who gets hurt in the process.

If you do end up getting into one of these relationships, it can be devastating. The dark manipulator is really skilled at using the dark seduction techniques to get what they want. They will find a victim who is vulnerable, and they will present the right solution that the victim needs at that time. For example, they may find a victim who just got out of a major relationship, and they will step in to feel the need of that victim to not be lonely any longer.

The seducer is going to be charming, fun, and the perfect person for that victim. The victim may feel like they have found their soulmate, but the seducer is just there to get what they want out of the relationship. Sure, it may last for some time, but as soon as the victim is no longer meeting the needs of the seducer, the seducer will be gone.

This will leave the victim hurt and broken. They may have overly trusted the seducer (because the seducer is skilled at reading the victim and knew exactly what to do and say to gain that trust and get what they want), and now they are broken. They may go through depression and anxiety and even have trouble trusting others in the future.

Because of all these negatives that come with dark seduction, it is important to watch out for the signs. If you run into dark seduction with a narcissist or with a psychopath, it is even more important to watch for the signs. These individuals are not there to care about what the other person wants. They simply look out for themselves, they feel that they deserve what they want, and they don't have the capacity to care about how it is going to harm the other person.

Due to the way that the relationship was started, including the romance, attraction, the mutual feeling that you found a soulmate (all created by the seducer to get what they want), when things start to take a lot of wrong turns, it is likely to be too late for you, the victim, to walk away. This can be especially true if you went into that particular picture without a good idea of what you wanted in the relationship. Without this clear picture, you would not have the determination to walk away from that relationship when it didn't meet your expectations.

This is why you must always make sure that you know what you want to get out of the relationship before one begins. This will help you be prepared if the relationship becomes something else because you will be able to see when it is going away from your chosen course. You will give yourself a chance to see it for what it is before you damage your self-worth so much where you will stay in that relationship and accept the bad treatment.

This can be hard. Many times we feel that we need a relationship like we are not worth anything unless we are in a relationship with someone else. Then, when we are not in a relationship, we are going to feel like something is missing, and we jump into the first relationship that comes available. This is where the issues will start.

Before you jump into the next relationship, it is important to take some time to soul search. Remember that there is nothing wrong with not being in a relationship all the time. Taking some time for yourself and really exploring where you are at that time in your life and what you would like to happen in your next relationship can make a difference.

This gives you a good idea of what kind of relationship you want to be in. You won't just jump into the next relationship because you are needy or because you worry about being alone. You will have specific goals in mind, and if you feel the relationship isn't going in the right direction, you will be able to step out before the dark seducer gets too deep and tries to take control over you.

The first thing that you should do here is to start with some deep thinking and even some soul-searching and decide on the details of the relationship that you are looking to enjoy at that time in your life. Describe what you want out of the other person in this partnership. Describe how you want to feel in this relationship. Set out some clear boundaries and then make sure that you understand why you have these boundaries.

Chapter 11: Ways That You Can Predict Other's Minds

You are an expert in beginning psychology now! Since you know all the ways that others might have hurt you, it's now time to take this power and do something good with it. No matter what you might have thought about your brain and your abilities in the past, you understand now that you have so much power that you were just given since birth. These abilities are not easily used. Some people will struggle to ever figure out who they really are and what they want from this life. You might still not know that, and that's perfectly fine. You shouldn't keep yourself perfectly labeled in a box or else this is going to limit your thinking. Whatever others have made you feel in the past does not define who you are now. Learn from your past and don't forget who you are or where you came from. Let go of the hurt you have felt so that you can start healing and moving forward in a more positive direction.

Make sure that you really get to know people. Don't make assumptions. The better that you can really understand a person and who they are at their core, the easier it will be to have a more positive influence over them. Even when you are feeling like you have no idea what you're doing, you can always do some digging internally and externally to discover a greater, more meaningful truth. If you start to make too many assumptions and only allow people to be the labels that you have put on them, this is really going to limit your abilities to grow and understand the world better.

Communication is going to be how it all happens. It is always going to be better to just lay the truth out there and talk it out rather than trying to hold onto things so deeply. Though it might be really scary and challenging, it is going to make you feel so much better in the end when you can speak your truth and let others hear your opinions and feelings. Don't try to persuade in other ways besides communication. Don't withhold things from people, such as something they might need. You can manipulate others this way, but communication and talking things out is going to be more effective and have longer-term results.

The hurt that you have felt can be used for good now. All you have experienced has led you to right where you are in this moment.

The darkest moments that you have gone through that you thought never would end are over now. The times when you wanted to run away and get rid of all of this have brought you to the person that you are now. Though you might never want to go back and do it over again, you should still learn to be grateful for these experiences, because without them, you wouldn't be able to be positively influential person that you are about to become.

Getting to Know Them

Now it is time in the book to start to do the thing that you probably want to more than anything – persuade others! We live in a world where influence is essential. If you can't manage to persuade certain people, then it can keep you back from achieving the things that you really want in this life. The most important thing that you will want to do is get to know who you are trying to persuade. Whether you want to convince your husband that you're ready to have children, or you want to persuade your entire 100-member sales team that they need to push harder to drive sales, it all starts with really getting to know who they are and how they operate.

The first step in this process is to look at their background. How old are they?

What gender do they identify as? Where do they live? What are their strengths? What are their weaknesses? What do they have already? What is it that they want? When you can answer these kinds of questions, it will become much easier to know how to come up with a plan of persuasion in order to suit your favor.

Certain kinds of differences will be important in this situation. For example, asking your 18-year-old boyfriend for $20 is going to be done in a different way than you would ask your 80-year-old grandmother for the same thing. In order to persuade people, you have to really understand the things that generically define them and then get into their deeper characteristics, such as things that create the personality that they have.

Next, you will want to determine what their likes are. What things make them happy? These should be easy to understand for people that you already know. When it comes to trying to analyze your customer base if you are trying to persuade sales, then think of basic things they'll like such as discounts, freebies, and other little rewards for being a consumer.

After you have managed to determine what it is that they might like, you should next try and figure out the things that they aren't as big of fans of. This might include things like long return times after purchasing something, having hidden fees, or not being able to customize their products. When you can identify both the things that they like and dislike, then it is easy to act accordingly. For everything that you might have that they will dislike, offer up a solution by providing something that they like. It seems so obvious, but a lot of people who try to influence others will completely disregard this.

Finally, make sure that you are highly aware of the way that they communicate. If you are understanding of this, it will be that much easier to make sure that you are expressing things with them in the same way. Always listen to the other person and ensure that you are giving them a platform to speak. Don't just look at the words they're saying but also their face as they start to share information with you.

If someone feels as though they aren't being listened to, it will make them want to turn away from you and they will be far less likely to be persuaded in the end. The next section is going to discuss further the importance of communication and how you can better enable this kind of healthy interaction in your life.

Understanding the Importance of Communication

Communication isn't easy for everyone. It seems so simple to just open your mouth and start talking. We all do it, sometimes with others, often alone, and sometimes without even thinking before we do start chatting away. It's not uncommon to find that you are struggling to share what you are feeling through the use of your words, even though you are currently experiencing that kind of emotion. The better you are able to communicate, the easier your life is going to be, and the happier you will become in the end.

To start off by bettering your communication skills, remember that it is a practice. There is no pill you can take or secret trick that you can start to do right now. You will have to make sure that you are practicing talking to other people in order to get better at it.

If you're just starting, practice first by having small conversations. This might be with a barista at your local coffee shop or someone at the bus stop as you both are waiting.

Don't bother other people, of course, but just look for ways that you can articulate your voice and try to say something beyond the basic "how are you?"

Make sure that you are effectively expressing your feelings to yourself. Sometimes when we are all alone we still won't fully understand what our emotions mean. If you have to, start journaling your feelings every day. The more that you can work them out yourself and write down the emotions that you are feeling, the easier it will be to work through them on your own. How can you expect to effectively share these with others if you aren't sure how to share them with yourself?

When it comes to starting to persuade others, ensure that you are careful with your words. You never want to force anyone to do anything or put them in a place where they might feel as though they have little to know control. Avoid using phrases such as "You should do this." No one wants to be told what to do.

Talk about yourself first. It seems counterintuitive, but people will be more likely to respond by picking up on example rather than having you tell them what to do. For example, let's say that you want to persuade your spouse to start waking up earlier because you think it would help prevent the stress of being late every morning. Rather than saying something such as "You should start to wake up earlier," you can say something such as "I found that by waking up earlier, it's helped me to be a lot less stressed in the morning before work."

Let others believe that the idea is their own. They will want to believe that they were the ones to come up with this plan, not the other way around. Give them the chance to work through the plan on their own, and they can figure out their own positives and negatives. It will be a more effective persuasion when you are able to inspire it within other people rather than forcing them to believe something.

After this, ensure that you are careful of your own tone and body language. Create an atmosphere where they can be comfortable around you. The more calmness, love, and compassion that you can show to them, the easier it will be for them to relate to you. Sometimes we feel as though we need to be rigid and stern in order to get people to do what we want. This isn't the case at all! You should be kind and loving, and others will be much more receptive.

Last but not least, ensure that you are being very respectful of those that you are trying to persuade. You want to make sure that they feel comfortable with you, not as if they need to be ashamed or embarrassed around you. If someone says something stupid, no matter how dumb it sounds, don't make fun of them for it! Don't laugh at people or belittle them for their beliefs. Build others up and you will find that they have that same kind of respect in return.

How to Turn Negative Manipulation into Positive Persuasion

You should be an expert on basic level psychology now! Our motives, passions, actions, and everything else all start within our mind and manifest themselves differently in each and every person. In order to really get what you want from this life, you have to start to learn how to understand other people.

If you go through life completely blind to how the brain works, it will end up hurting you in the end.

Take all of the manipulation that you might have learned in the past and find a way to use it for good now.

All of the negative experiences that you have had can be lessons that taught you how not to treat other people. In order to turn negative manipulation into positive persuasion, you have to start by having a good intention behind what you might want to persuade others of. Whatever you might be trying to get from others should be something that mutually benefits the both of you. Listen to the other person and what they might need so you can come to a place where you both can compromise and get the same kind of positive benefits in the end.

Ensure that you are always checking in with the needs of others after your own. Of course, you should take care of yourself first, but if you go through this life unconcerned with how others feel, this isn't going to help you in the long run.

An influencer is a leader. If you have good ideas that you hope to instill in other people, and you want them to be able to benefit from the things that you know, then it's essential that you work on having positive leadership skills.

Other people are not tools for you. Others can help you, but you also have to help them in some way.

A good leader knows how to get people to do what they want, but at the same time, they are providing something beneficial to that person. You might be able to get someone to help you achieve your dreams, but they should also be a part of that journey. When you can realign yourself and center your beliefs around this system, you will be able to achieve anything.

Ensure that you are always talking about the "we" and using confidence when talking to others. They will be more inclined to listen when you are including them in this process as well.

The most important thing that you will have in this process is a growth mindset. When people limit their thoughts, they are limiting their potential in life. Keep up with different studies on persuasion, manipulation, and psychology in general.

Subscribe to a newsletter or magazine about the human brain in order to get a better understanding of how that powerful thing in your head can work.

Make sure to always check in with your health. If you are not taking care of yourself in all aspects, then this is really going to affect how your mind works.

As we get older, our minds will only become more challenging to manage, so we have to ensure we are preparing ourselves now. Keep an open perspective and practice listening to others. Never stop learning. The more you know, the more you will realize just how much you have left to learn.

Never use aggression and persuasion either. You might be able to make people do what you want by having them fear you, but this will only take you so far. If you really want people to respect you in the long run and be influenced by you forever, you should never use fear and scare them into believing what you have to say. The more compassion and understanding that you have for other people, the more likely they will be to listen to all that you have to share.

Chapter 12: If You Get Caught

If you will truly advance your skill as a manipulator, you must know how to prevent yourself from getting caught. Recovering yourself from getting caught is a skill all on its own, and when done right you can actually put yourself right back into the position of being able to manipulate the person all over again. Many people are unaware of the necessary action required if you get caught. The reality is that recovering yourself is easy, but it is also a delicate process. You have to be very intentional and specific about how you do it, or you may end up burying yourself further and making it impossible for you to recover. Then, you lose your trustworthiness and credibility and may even tarnish your reputation, further damaging your ability to manipulate anyone in the future. If you get caught, follow these steps.

Stay in Control

You have to start by staying in control of yourself. Do not allow nervousness or fear to translate into how you are expressing yourself.

Keep your voice and body language strong and confident, even if you know that you have already been caught. Immediately switching into a defensive or nervous tone of voice and posture will result in you contradicting everything that you will say in the next step. This means that, no matter how well you say it, you will likely lose the trust and respect of the person that you are trying to manipulate. This will result in a complete failure and loss of your chance of effectively manipulating this person ever again.

Staying in control may be hard, especially if you tend to be an expressive or nervous person. For that reason, you want to really take action on this step. Do not even let yourself switch into nervous mode. Instead, keep your posture very strong and true to what you have already been doing, maintain your tone of voice and your vocabulary, and stay completely in control of yourself. The best thing you can do is let the nervous thoughts out of your mind so that the panic does not take over. You can do this by releasing the idea that you are caught and instead believing that you are about to regain control through your self-discipline. You are not caught. You are simply being questioned.

You are only truly caught if the person walks away convinced that you are a manipulative person. Until that happens, you are still in control. Period.

Completely Stop Trying

The next step is to completely stop trying to manipulate this person. You need to pull back entirely on every single level. Do not use any intentional persuasion, attempt to relate to them, or any form of manipulative request on them at all. At this point, they will be looking for evidence that suggests that you truly are manipulating them. For now, all they have is a suspicion. Your job is to keep it as a suspicion so that you can get them off of your trail and convince them that you are not, in fact, manipulating them.

Once you have entirely thrown the breaks on your attempts, you want to give in to what they are saying. Do not under any circumstances admit to manipulation. Never should you ever say "I agree," "Yes I was," or "You are right" to the fact that you are manipulating them. This immediately makes you guilty, and you cannot come back from that. Admitting directly to manipulating will not revive you or make it seem like you were at least being honest in the end.

This is not what it will look like to your target. Instead, they will think that had they not caught you, you would have never admitted what you were doing, and you would have manipulated them all the way until the end. Which, of course, you would have.

Instead of admitting to manipulating, you need to admit to understanding how they could think that. Period. You are never admitting to anything more than this. "Yes, I can see where you are coming from, but I assure you that is not what I was doing." "I understand what you mean, and I see how it likely felt that way, I'm sorry that I made you feel that way." Using admission to the illusion of manipulation but not to manipulation itself is a great way to apologize without pinning yourself as guilty. Then, because you admitted to understanding where they were coming from (and not to manipulation), they are more likely to begin to redevelop their trust in you again.

Slowly Get Back on Track

After you have admitted to understanding how your actions may have made them feel and you have apologized, you want to start slowly getting back on track with your manipulation.

The key word here is slowly. You do not want to rush this. You already had them suspicious and skeptical about you once, you do not want to get to that place again. This time, you need to be extra cautious and make sure that you are extremely careful not to get them suspicious of you again. Coming back once is easy, coming back twice is tough, and coming back three times is impossible. You never want to go past the first come back.

You should start by building relatability again. Share authentic stories, agree with the person you are talking to, and use this as an opportunity to rebuild the connection that you had going with you. As long as you do this effectively, it should not take long for you to rebuild the connection. Since you already had one prior to the accusation and the accusation was never affirmed as true, the person will likely find it easier to connect with you the second time around.

Once you have built relatability and begun persuading again, you can then move on to an easy manipulation tactic. The best one when recovering from nearly being caught is the Starting Small strategy, as you can slowly request more and more of the person so that they get used to saying yes to you again.

This also allows you to see how they respond to your requests so that you can easily gauge the size of the next request based on their response to the last one. Then, you can also determine exactly when to ask the big request so that it comes across as authentic and not manufactured. Remember, you don't want to get them suspicious of you again, especially not on your big request.

Seal the Deal

Once you get to the point where you feel that everything is flowing back on track again and everything is running smoothly, you can get back to seal the deal. Carry on just as you would have had you never been accused, but stay very cautious along the way. Cover your trail, act authentically, and do not make it obvious that you are in any way manipulating them to agree with you. That way, you can easily seal the deal with them.

The biggest key when you are manipulating someone is to refrain from dropping into "guilt mode."

You do not want to try to make them feel guilty, nor do you want to deny the person's feelings.

Trying to make the person feel guilty will make them look right, as we tend to become defensive when we are guilty of something ourselves. Saying things like "You really think that about me?" or "Do you really think I would do that?" or "I can't believe you would say that about me!" or anything else that would try and place the blame on them makes it apparent that you are feeling guilty about something. They will immediately think that you are guilty of manipulating them and then they will lose trust in you.

Denying what they are saying also won't work. People do not like to have their feelings denied, and that is exactly what you are doing if you deny manipulating them. That is why when you admit to the situation you say "I admit that I understand why you might feel that way, I'm sorry." You are admitting to respecting their feelings and validating that they have the right to feel however they are currently feeling. This assures them that you respect them and that you honor their feelings, thus immediately re-establishing their trust in you.

The difference between an immature and inappropriate response to being caught and a mature and proper response to being caught is that the immature and inappropriate response will keep you caught. Executing the mature and proper response will keep you undercover and allow you to carry on doing whatever it is that you were doing in the first place, only more secretive this time around!

Conclusions

Psychological warfare has been around for thousands of years. It has been used to instill fear in the enemy, create high or low morale, to intimidate, or even to inspire whole nations and mobilize soldiers. The best and effective kinds of psychological warfare is when the target doesn't even realize it. From Ancient civilizations to the Cold War, to the War on Terror. Psychological warfare has used techniques and tools based on the study of human behavior and thinking. The brain can be a powerful weapon and a weakness if properly manipulated both in and offensive and defensive way.

You may have also seen some techniques or practices a person in your life has used on you or others. When looking over certain accounts of archetypical people who use certain techniques or practices, could you relate because you have used the same techniques? Maybe, you have realized that you may have been taken advantage of by someone who has used these techniques on you. If you feel surprised, excited or even guilty, you are not alone. This book is not meant as a way to only "call out" faults or inform you on how to be aware of those who may take advantage of you or to only just instruct you on how to apply these techniques for selfish gains. Its purpose was to give you a rounded introduction into the realm of the study of dark psychology, techniques used in dark psychology, how to use some of these techniques and how to defend yourself for practitioners. It was only a taste of what dark psychology is.

Some of us have certain aspects of these skills or techniques ingrained in our lives and it has dictated our thoughts, actions and behaviors, we have in most cases readily used these skills from time to time. We just couldn't identify or notice these techniques or tools when they were being used, until we were informed of these techniques, much like how this book has probably informed you. Some of us didn't realize that we are a "triangulator", "blaster", or a "projector", maybe even a "flirt". At the time we used some of the techniques. At the time, using them just seemed natural, as though it was instinctual. For some of us, these skills are as natural to us as breathing. Certain techniques may have become habitual through experiences in our environment, such as watching people close to us like a family member, friend or a significant other. Perhaps we saw a person we would consider a role model or a celebrity we admire use the exact same technique.

As human beings, we can have a need to feel a certain level of contentment. It is through this contentment that we can feel comfortable. We can feel this urge to find this contentment while at home, at school, or at work. When people, places or things impede on that contentment, we will react. Sometimes, we will learn from these situations or events on how to react the next time something impedes on our contentment again, either emotionally or methodically. Our behaviors and thoughts, as

well as how we react to them can be no different as how an animal reacts in the wild: A skunk, when feeling agitated, lifts its tail and shoots out an unpleasant liquid. A bear will stand on its hind legs when it is ready to attack. For humans this is no difference.

You may have read about certain personality traits that use some of these dark psychological techniques, such as the narcissist or Machiavellian and related to some of their actions or behaviors.

If you feel guilty or upset, please try not to feel bad. We may have behaviors that are triggered when certain current experiences have mirrored others from our past.

Some of our behaviors and reactions are natural to keep us safe such as recoiling from a hot stove or feeling slightly uneasy when we are on top of a building looking down. Others are learned and can be directly linked to our past. It is up to us whether or not we want to make these thoughts or behaviors go away or reinforce them.

Maybe, this book has been informative in this.

Suppose you would like to know how to use these techniques in your personal life for you own gain. We are ambitious by nature. Like was stated earlier, we all want to feel a sense of comfort and contentment in our world. Maybe you want more than what is considered enough for contentment. Envy and jealousy can be powerful motivational feelings. Suppose you may want to get into management at your office, want to build up your confidence in a conversation or debate, or maybe you want to attract that special someone you have had your eye on and want to get and keep their attention. Maybe you really want to be the "alpha" and be feared and respected by your colleagues and friends. You may want to achieve your goals by any means. Again, that is entirely up to the individual on how to use the information in this book.

As we have seen, the study of human psychology and the term "dark psychology" is very broad and has many interpretations about its areas of study.

If one goes onto the internet, and simply type "dark psychology" in the search bar, they will be bombarded by various blogs, websites, books and videos on all of the topics outlined in this book, which may be in better detail. Many researchers have spent their entire lives studying and demonstrating these techniques, which this book only barely discussed. The internet, much like any informative resource, comes with an almost subconscious "buyers beware" warning label. While there are many experienced and dedicated researchers, there are also people who claim to have working experience and have their own experiences and theories in dark psychology, particularly in manipulative and persuasive techniques. While everyone is certainly entitled to their own opinion and experience when it comes to this field of study, it is up to you, to form your own opinion and experiences should you choose to continue researching dark psychology.

"Dark psychology"

Its name alone can illicit negative thoughts and aversion from this subject. Just as much as there are varying opinions about the usefulness and "positive"

review of the particular normal techniques in psychological therapy, such as neuro-linguistic programing (NLP) or cognitive behavioral therapy (CBT), there are just as many varying opinions about these same therapies being used for their "dark" purposes, as though the word "dark" should naturally be evil. "Dark" has always been associated with evil. A whole book could probably be written on that very subject. With the term "dark therapy", its uses can be used for anything. It is really in the hands of the user. Almost any part of psychology can be used in a negative way. Cults have used aspects of CBT and NLP to control and manipulate their followers and break their defenses down, so they are vulnerable and open to suggestion. Various world governments use certain stealth mind control techniques to hold their people in check and destroy dissension. There are so- called "experts who announce their experiences of understanding the ways of manipulation and can teach others so they can achieve their goal of "getting anyone into bed" or "getting anything you want".

Just as the study of dark psychology can be used in abusive ways, but it can also be used in helpful ways.

Subtle manipulation may sound evil, but how many times have we been affected by manipulation, only to see that it was beneficial for us in the end? Teachers have used positive reinforcement to build their student's confidence and used repetition in their lessons so their students can better retain what was taught. Parents have used the technique of recipocracy to get their kids to do chores, which in turn can build their mental and behavioral development, such as understanding the value of hard work if this is action is repeated over and over.

There are also those who use covert persuasion and manipulation in sales who honestly want to make sure they are able to find the product that would best suit their customer's wants and needs, as well as restaurant servers who make sure their customers they are getting taken care of, while the servers themselves are properly being tipped for their service. Dark CBT or NLP or the principles of influence can be used by management to help correct employee behavior and motivate employees to be more productive and positive. Companies have used rhetoric in their offices to inform employees of goings on within the company and to promote important details and regulations that would be seemingly uninteresting and mundane.

We can definitely use dark psychology to our advantage in our daily lives and get not only what we want, but we can also benefit others.

What is the next step? The next step is to continue on with researching dark psychology in all of its areas of study and techniques. Within time, you may find on technique or a combination that you are comfortable with and use them in your daily life.

All it takes to see the "dark side" of dark psychology and see that it isn't necessarily bad takes an open and keen mind. Understanding and mastering dark psychology isn't something to be afraid of. What is important when studying dark psychology is understanding your own intent. We must also be aware of the consequences when we are using these techniques. It can lead to success and gain, tangible or not. It can also lead to distrust, poor business habits, loss of relationships. The list can go on. As human beings, as we go out into the world, we have the ability to inspire or harm based on our behaviors, thoughts and actions. If you use these techniques wisely and effectively, you can get what you want.